AMENDING DREAMS

4/3/2021

Betty

Keep looking for signs of John. They can be in many places.

[signature]

AMENDING DREAMS

✦

Reflections and Meditations of a Widow

Joyce M. George

iUniverse, Inc.
New York Lincoln Shanghai

AMENDING DREAMS
Reflections and Meditations of a Widow

iUniverse books may be ordered through booksellers or by contacting:

iUniverse
2021 Pine Lake Road, Suite 100
Lincoln, NE 68512
www.iuniverse.com
1-800-Authors (1-800-288-4677)

ISBN-13: 978-0-595-36913-3 (pbk)
ISBN-13: 978-0-595-81325-4 (ebk)
ISBN-10: 0-595-36913-8 (pbk)
ISBN-10: 0-595-81325-9 (ebk)

Printed in the United States of America

This Book Is Dedicated To:

My loving husband and best friend of 28 years, Damian. His passing offered me guidance and strength to complete this mission. Thank you, dear hubby.

This book is also dedicated to you. May you proceed more quickly and smoothly through the grieving process with the recognition that you are not alone.

My daily prayers are for all widows and widowers to accept their new life and live it in the spirit of new hope and amended dreams.

Contents

Introduction xiii

Embrace Death and the Spiritual Life 1

Dinner for One. 4

Balancing Bills and Income 8

Depression 12

If Only… 15

Sorting My Guilts 18

Hug the Child Within 22

Fulfilling the Need for a Companion 25

Laughter During Grief 28

Return to Work After the Funeral. 31

Widowhood 35

Invading His Privacy. 38

Forgive Your Spouse 41

Journaling. 44

Talk With Others 47

To Pick Up the Pieces or Toss Them Out? 50

I Wish I Could… 53

Give Yourself Permission to Relax and Enjoy Living 57

Friends Come And Go. 61

Waves and Flood of Grief 65

Why Am I So Exhausted? 68

Finding My Special Gift 72

Obsessive Behavior 75

Look Alikes 78

Thank You, Lord, for My Faith. 80

Laughter in the Home 83

Why?. 86

Listening 89

Those Irritating Rubber Bands. 92

Were You Really As Happy As You Remember? 95

Our Hidden Inner Strengths 98

Allow Dreams to Form a Bridge 101

There is No Rush. 104

Power of Prayer 107

Allow Yourself to be Outrageous 110

Lending a Helping Hand or Ear to Others. 114

Transitioning. 118

Can I Love Again? 121

When Am I Ready to Risk Dating? 125

Regular Doctor Visits 129

It Has Been My Life Long Dream to. 132

Amending Your Dreams 135

Permission to Dance Again 139

Amending Dreams Workbook 142

- *Personal Information* 144
- *Burial Locations.* 146
- *Budget.* 148
- *Finances* 151
- *Medical.* 162
- *Legal Documents* 168
- *Insurance.* 170
- *Memorial/Burial Wishes.* 173
- *How Can I Simplify My Life?.* 176

Acknowledgments

I acknowledge my family, who has been a tremendous source of love and support, without whom this book would not have been possible:

My parents, June Antes Bianchi and John Bianchi, and John Antes (deceased)

My brother and sister-in-law, James Patrick and Johanna Antes

My children, who never cease to amaze me, and their respective spouse/spouse-to-be:

    Peter Damian and Kathleen Oberg George
    Suzanne Marie and Steven McNair
    Kathryn Elizabeth and James Heltzel
    Mary Allison and Todd Feiock
    Christopher John George and Shannon Gosman

My grandchildren, whose unconditional love fills my heart with joy:

    Ashley Marie Sherman
    Amber Irene George
    Zachary James Heltzel
    Jack Bailey Heltzel
    Tyler David McNair

Thank you to very dear friends, Kathleen Bauman, Sarah (Sally) and Richard Nicol, Lynn Farash, Marjorie Baker Price, Annette and John Bailey, Louise Valcourt, Tess Richard, Wendy Dale, Leanne Hale, Elizabeth Lyon, Linda Eames, Sue and David Wilson, Andy Cherre, Richard Hanford, Patricia Masters, Dawn Rindell, Leo J. and Cindy Kesselring. You have all been special earth angels and you each know how valuable your support has been to my family and me.

For his gentle encouragement and support, a special thank you to William A. Knight.

A very special thank you to Mary Holleran for her editorial assistance.

Introduction

While sitting in the office of the funeral home, I was listening to the stranger's voice offering suggestions as to whether I wanted to "embalm the body" or "cremate" it. My husband, my loved one, had become an "it." I wondered, "What am I doing here? I can't deal with this." It was surreal. My body felt like it did not belong to me—as if I was having an out-of-body experience.

When I say "I understand how you feel," I do. As you most likely have discovered, especially if you are a young widow, there are few who can truly relate to your grief and the *heavy* load that follows—the getting on with life. Well-intentioned family members, friends, co-workers and neighbors attempt to understand what it is like to be in your shoes, but it is impossible if they have not already experienced it themselves.

There are books for people who are single, engaged, newlywed, parents-to-be, parents, grandparents, girlfriends, but not enough about being a widow. That is why I have poured my thoughts and feelings into these pages. May your transition be made a little easier while reading this book—as I assure you that seemingly unusual thoughts and feelings are "normal." First, I have endured them. Secondly, through conversations with widowed friends and acquaintances, I have come to realize that we basically say the same things with perhaps different words.

While this book is for widows, it may be beneficial for any person enduring the pain of separation—since the loss of any relationship is a death in itself and the stages of grief are similar. Therefore, please feel comfortable offering it to recently widowed, divorced and separated family members and friends. It is an equally valuable tool for family, friends, neighbors and employers, who could benefit by becoming more sensitive to the grieving process and developing an awareness of the physical and emotional changes that it entails.

At the beginning a quote from the Jerusalem Bible offers an opportunity for spiritual reflection on each topic. Similarly, each chapter ends with a prayer of gratitude or request for divine intervention. With thoughts and words scrambled, perhaps my words will lead you to find an appropriate prayer for your specific situation.

When I discovered my husband's body after a heart attack stole him away during the night, I felt like a child whose dog had been run over by a car. My best friend, confidant, lover, and companion left me—forever. No advanced warning. No goodbye. After the initial shock and grief, emptiness, fear and the "now whats" took over. The "now whats" are the purpose of this book. While I am a widow, who is speaking from personal experience, there is no doubt that all widows may recognize themselves in my stories.

Actually, I wanted to bury my head and make it all disappear—as if it never happened. That wouldn't work because it did happen. My husband died. I had to believe it and I had to accept this fact. I had to continue to live.

How I wished that I didn't have to work for a living. Then again, if I didn't work, I would be sitting at home all day, and I did not want to be alone either. Absolutely none of my choices were appealing. Frequently I found myself in the midst of this type of circular thinking. Therefore, it was time to separate the unreal world from the real one. Not an easy task when you feel in between worlds.

The revelation that my entire world changed in an instant left decisions to be made. Everything was overwhelming:

- Where do I begin?

- Our children are not seeing eye-to-eye about how to grieve and deal with their emotions. How can I help them with their grieving? Am I the best one to assist them right now?

- What do I keep? What do I throw away? What would my husband want each of the children to have?

- How will I survive financially?

- Should I live alone? Could I live alone—financially and emotionally?

- My car is unsafe—should I buy a new one? Which make? Who should I/could I trust? Where should I go?

- How do I cook for one person? How do I get motivated to shop, to cook and to eat?

- What are my goals? ("Our" anticipated retirement goals disintegrated with his death.)

- Will our couple friends still include me?

- How will I plan for a one-person retirement?

- What should I invest in?

- Where will I go for entertainment? What can one person do alone for fun? Can I experience fun again?

- Will I take a vacation? Where? With whom?

- Will I feel like laughing, singing and dancing again?

Your list of "now whats" will be as endless as mine. In the past number of years I have found answers to some of these questions, which I share in the pages that follow. Other questions remain and that is okay. There is no deadline for resolving all of the issues.

This is a good time to begin making this book your own. Following each chapter, including this Introduction, is space for you to jot down your thoughts and feelings, problems and questions. At a later date, an unconscious thought may surface concerning something you have written and provide you with direction or answers. Hopefully, this will also be an opportunity to start writing, if you haven't already done so.

As I looked back into my childhood, it seemed that when a grandparent died, the remaining grandparent simply went on like nothing changed. The widow wore black for a year to symbolize her "period of mourning." Were they stronger people than we are? Was their faith deeper? I don't believe the answer is an affirmative one. However, people did not question as we do today. They accepted death as a fact of life and just went on with what needed to be done. As with their religion, they accepted what was told to them and did it. That's what I realized I needed to do: get on with living. It was tough.

I recommend that you keep *Amending Dreams* near your comfortable chair to browse through from time-to-time. May your fingers glide to whatever topics happen to tug at your heart. I will be with you, like a good friend whenever you need her to share experiences and encourage you to look inside yourself. These anecdotes and prayers have developed over a five-year period of time and for that reason not all of the topics will be of interest at this stage of your grieving process. Through these readings, may you connect with the spirit of your creator and that of your spouse as you continue on your journey called *life*.

Though you may not believe it now, there will come a time when you will feel like amending your now shattered dreams. Taking the steps to amend the first dream will be a very special one in your healing process.

Should you wish to share your thoughts or comments with me, feel free to e-mail me at jmag1017@yahoo.com. I would enjoy hearing from you.

Embrace Death and the Spiritual Life

The virtuous man, though he die before his time, will find rest.
Length of days is not what makes age honourable,
nor number of years the true measure of life;
understanding, this is man's gray hairs,
untarnished life, this is ripe old age.
He has sought to please God, so God has loved him;
as he was living among sinners, he has been taken up.
He has been carried off so that evil may not warp his understanding or
treachery seduce his soul;
for the fascination of evil throws good things into the shade,
and the whirlwind of desire corrupts a simple heart.
Coming to perfection in so short a while, he achieved in life;
his soul being pleasing to the Lord,
he has taken him quickly from the wickedness around him.

—Wisdom 4:7–14

As a child, I recall the death of relatives being whispered about among the adults. It was as if death was a big secret that needed to be kept from the children. We were not allowed to go to the funeral home or the funeral itself until we were adolescents. This instilled many fears in me. Fear of the unknown. Fear of death taking someone I loved away forever. Fear that someday I would be swiped away from my family to an unknown destination, never to return.

As my favorite philosopher, Leo Buscaglia, told us in *Personhood—The art of being fully human*, we must enjoy the quality of our life now on earth as if the "tomorrow" we wait for will never come.

Death indicates that our work is done that the Lord had a list of things for us to accomplish and we completed the tasks for which we were placed on earth.

1

Our reward, for those who believe in life ever after and the Lord, is that our soul lives forever in God's loving embrace. What more could we want!

For me, listening to psychic mediums, such as John Edward, James Van Praagh and Sylvia Browne gives me a positive image of the life hereafter. Through their communications with the spirits of the deceased, they offer reassurance that our loved ones watch over us. We are told that our loved ones give us messages to let us know of their presence—making an object move, turning on lights, leaving their scent in a room.

We can learn how to tune in to our loved one's spiritual energy and feel their presence. This happened to me as I was preparing to move to my condo from a townhouse that I rented for a few months. It was an extremely tense time—a giant move, which was both terrifying and exciting. I was not used to making decisions alone, so I worried about whether it was the right move for me. I was standing in the kitchen of my home about two weeks before the scheduled move and my left forearm felt as if someone was ever so lightly stroking it. The static electricity made the hairs on my arm straighten and wave. This sensation occurred on three consecutive days while I was making dinner. It was spooky. After the third time, it occurred to me that it was my husband letting me know that everything was going to be okay. I couldn't help but laugh when I figured that out. And I said out loud, "Thank you, Damian. I know you are here with me." The stroking stopped. However, he has made his presence and his assurances known to me in my dreams on of a number of occasions.

Recently I lost my job and was nervous about my financial future. It had been months since I heard from my husband in a dream and I was quite surprised when he appeared one night. Through his silent presence and a warm hug, he let me know that he was watching over me—that I would find a job and that I was not alone. He was correct. Within a few weeks I answered an employment advertisement that I found in our local newspaper, interviewed and was hired by a law firm where the attorneys and staff create a warm and caring environment.

Dear Lord,
While I do not comprehend the vastness of the spiritual world, I am grateful for the opportunities to still see, hear and feel the presence of my husband in my dreams. Thank you for making his presence known to me. May I ask that you take good care of him until we meet again. Thank you, Lord. Amen.

My thoughts:

Dinner for One

Eat honey, my son, since it is good;
honey that drips from the comb is sweet to the taste;
and such is knowledge of wisdom for your soul:
find it, and there will be a morrow,
and your hope will not be in vain.

—Proverbs 24:13, 14

Those first meals alone were right at the top of my Most Difficult Adjustments List. First of all, I experienced no pangs of hunger. Perhaps for the first time in my life food meant nothing. Often nausea would strike before I processed the fact that my body needed nourishment. I had to eat, I had to go on with life. A banana, a piece of toast or a handful of nuts were often the foods that were easy to grab and munch on to satisfy my mind's habit at mealtimes.

For about three months, I'd walk into the kitchen and stand there—totally blank. Absolutely nothing popped into my mind. I would simply stare at the wall. Total numbness filled my entire being. When I forced myself to concentrate on thinking about making a meal, nothing would come to mind—which was probably a good thing since the cupboards were fairly bare. I had no ambition to grocery shop, as to muster up that much energy was not worth it.

Eventually I ventured out to local restaurants. Initially, I chose restaurants that my husband and I had not frequented, to prevent the painful memories that triggered the flood of tears. Eating alone in a restaurant was quite difficult, but less so than eating alone at home. As I looked around, I had plenty of company in that there were a number of solo diners at other tables. My aching heart dearly missed my dining companion. I tried reading a book while awaiting my food, but I couldn't even concentrate enough to follow the words. Generally, I just let my mind wander, as it would anyway. My thoughts were like trying to lasso a wild horse. There was no way to get them to settle down and relax so that I could get a hold of them. "This must be a stage," I told myself. And it was, and it passed.

4

When I found myself starving for a good, old-fashioned, home-cooked meal, it was time to get to the grocery store and buy the ingredients. At first, I phoned one of my daughters and asked if I could go shopping with her. Grocery shopping was never an enjoyable chore, and now it was even less so and any way I could dress it up to make it more appealing made sense to me. She always brought along my grandson, and we would make a game of finding items in the aisles. And, I always bought a bouquet of fresh flowers to put on my dining room table.

Widows often have difficulty focusing on one thing because there are so many things to handle all at once. For that reason, a widow can become a very good self-therapist. By this I mean, for example, I forced myself to sit down and write answers to my questions. "How can I make cooking and dining appealing to me?" Once I learned to focus on that one question, the answers flowed: play a favorite CD and turn up the volume a couple of notches; open the blinds to invite in the natural sunlight; set the table with placemats or tablecloth, flowers, and good china; make the foods I enjoy, like stuffed peppers, spaghetti and casseroles, and plan to eat at a regular time. Would you believe, the toughest decision I faced was whether to use the tomato-based sauce or the beef bouillon-based sauce for the pasta? The beef bouillon won when I added onions, peas and ground beef. Another idea was to prepare a list of friends and relatives to invite to dinner and to pencil them in on my calendar. After entertaining my first few dinner guests, cooking wasn't such a dreaded chore.

Recently I made old-fashioned bread pudding with raisins—my favorite—which took me back to when all five children were living at home. None of them would get close enough to even smell the pudding. After decades of cooking for a family of seven, and usually one or more guests, I needed to cut the recipe down to 2–3 servings. Delightfully, now when I get ambitious enough to bake bread pudding, I have enough for a few days, and enjoy every bite.

Accents such as a lit candle—a scented one like vanilla, raspberry or blueberry adds to the pleasantness of the meal—even when dining alone. Between the candle's fragrance and that of the floral bouquet, I was my own special guest. While it may sound sad, I found it to be very uplifting.

With the preservation packets that come with bouquets of flowers, I discovered that I could keep them fresh for two weeks. I'd use one-half packet when I brought them home. At the end of that first week, I cut off about a half-inch from each stem, run them under fresh water to remove any decaying leaves, emptied the other half of the packet in a freshly cleaned and water filled vase. Voila. I had fresh flowers for the second week of dining pleasure.

One thing I neglected to mention was the chore of finding a recipe that's right, a chore because my brain was on overload and just didn't want to function, even a simple thing like cooking familiar dishes became a task. By getting my recipes together and going through them once, then either marking the ones I liked with paper tabs, or putting favorite recipes in the front of the card box, they were easier to access. I made a list of the food staples necessary to have on hand for these recipes, and found this activity stimulated my interest in grocery shopping and in cooking.

With a sprinkle of dinner guests here and there throughout the month, the cooking juices got stirred up, and those mealtimes were special treats to me, disguised as treats for my guests. In return, I would receive reciprocal dinner invitations extended to me. Ahh, one less meal for me to think about.

Dinner for one, while no longer a sad experience, will most likely never be a favorite one for me. Rather, it becomes just another adjustment in life.

Dear Lord,
I am grateful for having had the meal companionship of my spouse for as long as You gave us together. Thank you for all the blessings I currently have, though You may need to continue to remind me that they are blessings. I recognize You in the smile of a stranger, a kindness of a neighbor or an acquaintance, and the note from someone I haven't heard from in years. Thank you, again, dear Lord. Amen.

My Thoughts:

Balancing Bills and Income

Listen to advice, accept correction,
to be the wiser in the time to come.

—Proverbs 19:20

Organizing bills and money was never my forte. It was something I had not done in almost three decades. My husband always took care of the finances—it was the man's thing to do, so I was told. Suddenly, I was faced with the fact that I had no choice. I had to learn quickly and begin writing checks. But where and how?

After procrastinating as long as I dared, I sat down with all the bills and prepared a list. After all, I needed to know exactly what had to be paid and when, the balances owed and what the monthly payments would be. My list included:

√ Telephone (monthly)

√ Cell Phone (monthly)

√ Heating/Electric (monthly)

√ Mortgage/Rent (monthly)

√ Gasoline for Automobile (weekly)

√ Groceries (weekly)

√ License Renewal (annually)

√ Car Inspection (annually)

√ Car Insurance (annually or monthly)

√ Homeowners/Renters Insurance (annually)

√ Medical Health Insurance (monthly)

√ Homeowners Association Fees (monthly)

√ Income Taxes (annually)

√ Furnace/Air Conditioning cleaning/inspection (annually)

√ Car Maintenance (per maintenance schedule)

√ Charge cards (monthly)

√ Loans (monthly)

√ Gifts—birthdays, holidays, weddings, anniversaries, miscellaneous

√ Household items (as needed)

√ Clothing (as needed)

√ Cable Television

√ Internet

Next to each item I entered dollar figures based on prior bills. When I totaled the figures, I was shocked to realize the amount of money that I needed to maintain a budget and household. Next, I broke down all the figures into the frequency of payment: weekly, monthly, quarterly or biennially. Gradually, the full picture came into focus. My budget was set. There was no extra money left over, but I was able to exist without sweating about surviving financially.

From time to time I review my budget and make adjustments to allow, for example, for a vacation or a concert ticket. I changed my gas/electric company to get lower rates. I changed my telephone to metered service free of any frills. Now I may change my cell phone to my home telephone number and eliminate a home telephone bill, as I see more and more households are doing the same to economize. By going to basic cable and occasionally renting movies, I found that I save over $40 a month. And by purchasing paper products in bulk at Sam's Club or BJ's Wholesale Club, I get more for my dollar.

When I read the bi-annual literature I received from my furnace cleaning company, I learned that if I turn down my heat during the time I am not at home, raise it for the hours I am in the house, and then lower it at bedtime, I use less heat, which reduces the monthly bill. The same would be true with the air conditioner in the hot weather. Now when I compare my heating/air-conditioning bill with others, mine is generally the lowest.

Grocery shopping was the most difficult adjustment. I found myself throwing away too much food. After buying for a large family for almost 30 years, buying for one person was a puzzle. Through trial and error, I have managed to purchase smaller portions and shop more frequently. If I shop on my way home from work and buy what I will need for two or three days, I tend to use that food and waste less. If I invite guests to dinner, extra food is shared, and both preparing dinner and eating it is much more enjoyable.

Listening to other singles talk about finances gave me some useful tips and hints. Articles in the local newspaper, television shows and the Internet were other sources of financial information. I also read books on finances, saving for retirement and investing.

Some days I feel like I am always conscious of money. Perhaps this is because mine is now a single-income one-person household. Life has changed. I need to be aware of frivolous expenses; but on the other hand, I need to be able to enjoy living, too.

Another choice is to obtain the advice of an investment advisor/broker. I selected someone I knew and trusted. If you are not familiar with a person in the investment/banking fields, ask trusted friends, family members, or colleagues for a referral. They might be able to help you compile a list of questions you should ask the advisor. This could be of great benefit to you.

Lastly, it is important to read all the fine print in any materials sent with your bills, as well as the fine print of any contract or agreement. A salesperson can tell you anything, but what you sign is binding. The salesperson can just relax a bit while you take all the time you need to read that fine print that many don't pay much attention to. You should always know what you are signing and what you are agreeing to.

Dear Lord,
Please calm my fears about my financial future. Help me to trust in the people you bring into my life who can give me good advice and information. Also, Lord, I need the confidence to make such decisions. When I reach that point, I will then pray to you and ask for guidance to make the best choices. Thank you, Lord. Amen.

My Thoughts:

Depression

Raise me up when I am most afraid,
I put my trust in you;
in God, whose word I praise,
in God I put my trust, fearing nothing;
what can men do to me?

—Psalm 56:3, 4

We all know that depression is a constant state of feeling sad. If you have reached a point where it is impossible for you to manage on your own, you should speak with your doctor. With all the stresses and the fast-paced society we live in today, there are many people taking medication to control depression and anxiety. Years ago, there was a stigma attached to anti-depressant drugs. However, times have changed and this is no longer true.

Many of us do have a choice: To remain sad (not to remain sad). The answer lies in education. By educating myself as to what opportunities were available to help me with my inner conflict, I gained confidence in my ability to help myself. As with any problem, the first step is to recognize the sadness, depression or anxiety—whatever the case may be. The second step is to research the available resources—doctors, family, clergy, friends and even the library or Internet. The third step is to determine what two or three resources are best for you. The fourth step is to make the contact(s). The final step is to follow through on what you learned and determined best for you.

I chose to seek group counseling from a former alcohol treatment center co-worker. Through guided imagery, I was enabled to gain a new focus and perspective that brought clarity to my cluttered brain. This focus came from within my soul through the universal energy that ties the spiritual and physical worlds together. I read books by Sylvia Browne and James Van Praagh that explained the deceased spirit's connection between the two worlds. To know that my husband's spirit was alive and nearby enveloped me in a comfortableness that gave me the energy to forge ahead.

Meditation, imagery, relaxation exercises, and physical exercises are all ways to lessen depression and anxiety. The goal of each is to teach us how to focus—on a reading, on what we are hearing, or listening to the body. The first time I experienced guided imagery with my counselor, it was absolutely amazing how relaxed I became. I realized that I had never felt truly relaxed before. The joke was that I thought I came to the session in a relaxed state.

Friends, doctors and clergy should be familiar with the names of reputable practitioners in your community who will be able to explain and demonstrate each of these techniques. Groups are generally easier than one-on-one sessions, but that decision is up to the individual.

Researching information on foods and beverages would be another topic to investigate. Some foods and beverages increase sadness and depression, while others improve the conditions. I suggest you discuss this topic with your doctor or therapist, or to research on the Internet or at the library. And of course, light deprivation in some people can add to the degree of sadness they feel. This, too, may be an area to be investigated.

> Dear Lord,
> You are my light and my strength. Your guidance is more necessary now than ever. I trust that you will open my ears to hear what I need to help myself, open my ears to truly listen to what I am hearing, and give me the courage to follow through. You may need to give me a nudge from time to time to remind me that I am not alone—you are with me. Thank you, Lord. Amen.

My Thoughts:

If Only…

Wisdom is bright, and does not grow dim.
By those who love her she is readily seen,
and found by those who look for her.
Quick to anticipate those who desire her, she makes herself
  known to them.
Watch for her early and you will have no trouble;
you will find her sitting at your gates.
Even to think about her is understanding fully grown;
be on the alert for her and anxiety will quickly leave you.
She herself walks about looking for those who are worthy of her
and graciously shows herself to them as they go,
in every thought of theirs coming to meet them.

—Wisdom 6:12–17

If only I had tuned in to Damian's words and actions over his last six months of life, I may have been able to keep him alive at least for a bit longer. When I wanted to buy new drapes for the living room, he commented that in the Spring I would want to get drapes for the new house. What new house? We had discussed this possibility, but he wanted to remain where we were living, so I thought it was a closed issue. Instead of asking what he meant, I assumed he was open to house hunting but I didn't ask for clarification. Another clue should have been that he couldn't sleep well. After a couple hours of sleep, he would awaken feeling exhausted, but was unable to fall asleep. He said he was sleeping less and less. At the time, I didn't realize that was a sign of heart problems. A further flag should have risen when I mentioned the desire to attend college classes to obtain paralegal certification. We were at a point in our lives when we could finally come and go as we pleased. My attending classes would put a crunch in our freedom, but Damian eagerly and wholeheartedly supported my decision. In total, these instances indicate there was a problem and I was blind to it. If only I had listened attentively, perhaps life would have taken a different direction.

Hindsight is certainly not a gift. It haunts. It hurts. It reminds us that we are not perfect. Following the death of a loved one, we fall into the pattern of looking back. Perhaps it is from our need to learn from mistakes. Only in this case, I found that it serves no useful purpose. The end result is hurt and self-torture. There is no way possible to delve into the past and make any changes or corrections; no erasing allowed.

When the "If Onlys" creep into our lives, we would better care for ourselves by pushing them aside and remember instead the good times. By recalling the fun events, we cannot beat up on ourselves for anything we should have done, could have done better or would have handled differently, "if only I had known".

This is also a time to not allow others to encourage the "If Onlys" by telling them the past is over and cannot be changed. The only past you will tolerate is revisiting the enjoyable events.

> Dear Lord,
> I need your strength to not look backward in a negative way. Instead, guide me to seek answers to my current needs. Please help me to appreciate all that I have in my life and accept the present as the gift that it is from you. Amen.

My Thoughts:

Sorting My Guilts

My guilt is overwhelming me,
it is too heavy a burden;
my wounds stink and are festering,
the result of my folly;
bowed down, bent double, overcome,
I go mourning all the day

—Psalm 38:4–6

Yahweh, do not desert me,
do not stand aside, my God!
Come quickly to my help,
Lord, my saviour!

—Psalm 38:21, 22

On a hot day in July of 1971, Damian and I married. We had spent many hours discussing how our marriage would be—combining what we liked and did not like from each of our parents' marriages. I was the one who was nervous and concerned about the "what ifs." Damian was happy-go-lucky and optimistic. I suppose we balanced each other.

We added five children to our family within the first 8 years of marriage—which also added a tremendous amount of pressure on us financially and emotionally. It was mutually agreed that the mother should remain at home to care for the family and that is what I did. Here is where my first guilt came in: I felt guilty that I was not helping financially. This was totally unrealistic guilt, as it was physically impossible for me to work and take care of our children and household in a manner that would be fair to all of us. In addition, the cost of babysitters would have been more than I could possibly have earned. Yes, it was totally unrealistic guilt.

My husband handled the money throughout our marriage. During our 12th year, he came home one day announcing that he was let go from his job. While I knew it was devastating to us, I had no idea what we owed, or how much income we needed to survive. He paid the bills. Fortunately, he still had a part-time job delivering newspapers in the middle of the night, which brought in some money.

Damian ended up being out of a full-time job for a year. So, we reversed our daytime roles. He continued to deliver newspapers in the wee hours of morning. He stayed at home caring for the house and our children. I went back into the workforce. I had to work for my own mental well-being, as I refused to shop with food stamps like we had to do for a few weeks after Damian's layoff. However, as much as I enjoyed being with other adults and bringing home a paycheck, I felt guilty that I was the one working and not Damian. This was unrealistic guilt, as he was religiously seeking employment but had no bites. On the flip side, he truly enjoyed that year of being closer to our children.

We ended up losing our home, but the Lord sent an earth angel who found us a rental home where we had a new start.

Besides the fact that our children were bonding more closely with their father, another positive side of Damian being at home was that he sure could cook better than me. I'd say there was nothing to eat in the house, and he'd return from the kitchen a half-hour later with a fabulous meal! No, I wouldn't begin to feel guilty about my cooking—it was something I never was really taught and didn't enjoy.

After about a year, Damian landed a full-time day job and was able to quit delivering newspapers. What happened? His boss retired and Damian jumped into the boss' shoes and became manager of the newspaper deliverers. I remained employed, as our youngest child was four years old and in day care. Working meant security for me in my attempt to avoid ever having to go through such a tough year again. Luckily, that never happened again.

We remained in that house for the next 18 years. At times I felt guilty that our children were living in a rented house, but that unrealistic guilt would pass quickly. We were most fortunate to be able to keep our family together. Naturally, there were many good times, fun events with much laughter and singing intertwined with the rocky moments, like most marriages and families experience.

The last two or three years of his life, Damian became more stressed and the older he became and the more hours demanded of him at work, the shorter his fuse. To compensate and keep peace in our home for our children, I became the calmer, more optimistic one. I couldn't protect our children when their father misunderstood their actions or words as he verbally criticized them. This guilt still troubles me, as I don't know if it was realistic or unrealistic.

The rest of my guilt stems from now believing my husband's last couple of years could have been happier for everyone had I gone with him to doctor appointments and that he have a thorough physical examination. Perhaps this exam would have revealed his deteriorating medical condition and prevented his death or at least delayed it.

However, it wasn't until later that my adult children and I later put the pieces together and recognized that he had not been well those last two to three years. I could see he was aging rapidly, graying, and wanted to relax and sleep more. At other times, he couldn't sleep at all. Damian was diabetic, but to my knowledge, he never had any other health problems. Then on December 7, 1999, he went to his final sleep in the early hours of the morning while the rest of us were asleep.

I struggled with the guilt of not having made his life easier and less complex. I struggled with not having understood his short fuse. I struggled with the guilt of not having made his life happier, of not being a better wife, and of putting too heavy of a burden on his shoulders over the years. Some of it was realistic guilt but most of it was not. He was an adult and he made his own decisions. He could have followed his doctor's instructions instead of his interpretation of them.

The Lord is merciful and forgiving. I have asked for forgiveness from both the Lord and Damian for my wrongs. There is no doubt that I have been forgiven by both. The Lord loves us unconditionally, and I know Damian loved me dearly.

Another person who needed to be forgiven was myself. For what? There were the realistic guilts, my impatience with myself and my lack of confidence in what I could achieve. Too much personal energy had been wasted on negativity.

As my adult children continue to share their observations concerning my growth and my being an inspiration to them, my joy is in them and through them, as I continue molding a new life for me. This is proof to me of the forgiveness I've been shown by the Lord, by Damian, and by myself.

Facing guilts begins with listing them, then sorting them into groups—which are realistic and which are unrealistic. By processing these guilts and looking at them in an objective manner, you will be able to release them once and for all. I did it and you can do it, too. Be good, kind and loving to yourself as you forgive YOU, your spouse, and move on with living.

> Dear Lord,
> You have a plan for each of us. This I must trust. You allow us to make our own decisions. I cannot be responsible for those of my spouse or anyone else—just mine. Please continue to remind me to keep tuned in to the signs and whispers you give me as clues. Amen.

My Thoughts:

Hug the Child Within

People were bringing little children to him, for him to touch them. The disciples turned them away, but when Jesus saw this he was indignant and said to them, 'Let the little children come to me; do not stop them; for it is to such as these that the kingdom of God belongs. I tell you solemnly, anyone who does not welcome the kingdom of God like a little child will never enter it.' Then he put his arms round them, laid his hands on them and gave them his blessing.

—Mark 10:13–16

When a crisis arises, the child within stirs and old fears and worries rekindle. That little girl you once knew is still inside of you. Part of you matured and moved on with your life. The other part of you is locked inside. She can surface when buttons are pushed that remind you of scary events in your childhood. Perhaps it was parents fighting, someone trying to give you an uncomfortable touch, being scolded for misunderstood deeds, or feeling guilt over the death of a parent or sibling. It may even be feeling guilt because of your parents' failed marriage. Something can remind you of any of these events subconsciously and stir the little girl within. She gets scared and you feel it, but because it is your subconscious tugging at your heartstrings, you don't understand what is occurring.

My child within was fearful of loneliness. It was a scarey and uncomfortable feeling from childhood that had resurfaced. As a child brought up in a "do as I say" home, I frequently didn't understand what was happening around me or why. Children were not supposed to ask questions. Now as an adult I was facing this inner child who was panicking as she had not asked appropriate questions over the years. Here I was an adult with the fears of a child. The child wanted comforting and she wanted to have someone take care of her. Through meditation, I was able to calm down the inner child's fears. I told here that she was not alone as she has my children to assist us along with many friends and relatives. I gave her hugs and promised to take good care of her.

Take the time to sit or lie down and relax in total silence—no television, radio or distractions of any kind. Take a couple of slow, deep breaths and just be silent. Listen to what comes up. If nothing, ask your little child if she is hurting or scared and why. Wait and see what she answers. You may be very surprised with what feelings surface or memories renew.

If nothing happens, be patient and try it again another time.

If you do experience old feelings and memories, treat them in your adult manner as you would have liked them to be handled when you were a child. Reassure the little girl, tell her you love her. Envision hugging your child within and tell her you will always be there for her. Offer comfort and support.

Reaching such a level may be a foreign experience for you. It may be something you may wish to explore with a trained counselor for the first time(s) until you get the feel for what I am describing. You deserve the loving.

Dear Lord,
The child within gets scared and needs comfort from You to believe that she is safe. She needs to know that You will always be there and will never let her down. Please embrace her with your love now and forever. Thank you, Lord. Amen.

My thoughts:

Fulfilling the Need
for a Companion

I am the good shepherd;
The good shepherd is one who lays down his life for his sheep.
The hired man, since he is not the shepherd
and the sheep do not belong to him,
abandons the sheep and runs away
as soon as he sees a wolf coming,
and then the wolf attacks and scatters the sheep;
this is because he is only a hired man
and has no concern for the sheep.
I am the good shepherd;
I know my own
and my own know me,
just as the Father knows me
and I know the Father;
and I lay down my life for my sheep.

—John 10:11–15

Today, having a companion could mean another person, a pet, a weapon, or even the Internet. For me, it was inviting a puppy into my home and my life. (I already had the Internet.) After months of researching breeds, I chose a Bichon Frise, a small dog that was appropriate for condo living. A book on the breed indicated "bichons" enjoy entertaining, love children, and basically, enjoy life. That's what I needed. True to his breed, Trinket, as my grandchildren named him, was the perfect companion. He forced me to step outside my front door several times a day for a walk, where I would meet neighbors doing the same thing, as well as joggers, walkers, and passersby in cars, who would stop to chat about my puppy.

When you have a pet, I discovered that people are more trusting and open. Strangers would strike up a conversation, generally beginning with, "What kind of dog is that?" My adult children joked with me that Trinket was a "chick magnet" and my youngest son would volunteer to stop by and take Trinket for a walk in the park. All ages were drawn to my bichon, especially when he would parade around on his hind legs showing off. At times, his face even smiled—for real. Because of him, I met far more people in my new neighborhood than I ever would have met without my canine companion.

A puppy loves unconditionally. He needs and eagerly accepts love in return. I found he kept my mind busy so I had less time to live in the past. His antics made me laugh, and his energy kept me moving. My heart leapt with joy when Trinket cuddled, licked me or just laid by my side and kept me company.

Trinket filled the void that would have been painful without him.

Dear Lord,
Thank you for four-legged creatures to show us how to love and remind us how unconditional love is the best. Amen.

My thoughts:

Laughter During Grief

Kindly words are a honeycomb,
sweet to the taste, wholesome to the body.

—Proverbs 16:24

We started to laugh right from the day of my husband's death. It may sound outrageous and disrespectful, but it was not that way at all. My family agreed that Damian would have wanted to hear our laughter. As we shared stories about him, we could not contain the inner urges to bellow. Damian so loved to tell jokes, and the funniest part of the joke always was his bellyaching laughter to the point of tears rolling down his cheeks as he tried to find the voice to tell the punch line. Many people over the next few weeks shared their stories about his humor and joke telling.

As we roared with laughter, tears flowed freely. One took care of stress; the other washed some of the sorrow. In reliving our stories, we were united in the love and memory of a special man. And it made him present to us.

One of my adult children brought to the funeral home a video that Damian had made of himself as he practiced to perform a mime skit at a club party. After messing up what little hair remained on the top of his head, he disheveled his clothes, grabbed a toy guitar and mimed a 1970's comedian's song about his mother-in-law leaving (and taking his wife too). People who could handle viewing the video gathered around and were entertained by his performance. Those who could not endure the pain of watching him, steered away. They had a choice.

Damian's funeral was truly a celebration of the life of the man we were all there to remember and to show our love and respect.

I remember going to funeral homes over the years and watching people as they whispered, which I never understood. There is absolutely nobody to disturb. Perhaps other nationalities mourn differently, but the German-Irish adults in my life maintained the silence out of respect for the deceased. The younger generation gathered in a corner with the one family joker and delighted in his jovial recollections of the deceased. That was the celebration of that person's life. The funeral is

28

for the family and friends—to gather and deal with their loss. It is the final tribute to the person who affected their lives in various ways.

Subsequently, our family gathers on Damian's birthday and on the anniversary of his death to remember him in special ways. We generally unite in prayer at the cemetery. My grandchildren release balloons to "Papa." The joy in their eyes and faces and knowing they are sending their love in a special way brings tears to my eyes. We then gather for dinner and share our favorite stories and remembrances.

Dear Lord,
Laughter heals and the tears that accompany it are like salt on the potato chips. Thank you, Lord, for laughter, tears, and, yes, for potato chips, too. Amen.

My thoughts:

Return to Work After the Funeral

I gazed into the visions of the night,
and I saw, coming on the clouds of heaven,
one like a son of man.
He came to the one of great age
and was led into his presence.
On him was conferred sovereignty,
glory and kingship,
and men of all peoples, nations and languages became his servants.

—Daniel 7:13, 14

My return to work after my personal leave was a bittersweet experience. Since my husband had driven me to and from my downtown job for many years, simply driving was a tremendous adjustment, let alone downtown driving. For me to allow the car to go on automatic, so to speak, over the familiar route would not work for me. It was simply too painful.

As I selected my new route, a tape of Damian's words played in my head. "The side roads are safest." It was his belief that if something were to happen on the expressway, you could be stuck there for hours until help arrived, whereas on the side streets, you could walk to get assistance. However, it was time for me to make my own decisions. My conclusion was that the expressway was faster and safer and that someone was not going to attempt to jump into my vehicle (an experience I had as a new teenage driver while stopped at a traffic light). Making this decision was painless, and it felt rather freeing.

My bosses and co-workers had a difficult time welcoming me back. They politely asked as to how things were going, but it was frustrating because none of them could possibly realize what I was experiencing. I knew that they did not want to hear the truth when they asked, "How are you doing?" Inside my head, I was very angry that they each had a spouse to go home to, and I didn't. (My heart knew better.) "It isn't fair," I sobbed and wailed during my car ride home after hearing a co-worker complain about her spouse. Naturally, I felt she should go home and give her husband a smothering hug and realize her blessings, but my lips remained sealed, as it was not my place to lecture.

Radios were allowed at work. My tears flowed like an opened floodgate when a song with a special meaning to "us" was played. And just one time my boss, during a telephone conversation, burst into what I'd term a "fake" laugh, identical to that which my husband used to cackle (and they had never met one another). I froze in my chair. It was as if Damian used my boss to announce his presence to me. At other times, when people cracked a joke (Damian was a connoisseur of jokes) or a discussion ensued concerning the newspaper company (where he worked for 25 years), I held back the tears the best I could in the presence of others. There was no predicting what would trigger a tearful reaction.

Another day, my boss commented that I needed to "concentrate more" on my work. This took place less than six months after the most devastating event in my life. During this time, I was disposing of a 28-plus-year collection of "stuff," moving from our family home, separating our two remain-at-home young adult children because I could not afford a roof for both (one remained with me; the other went to live with her older sister and brother-in-law), attending college at night, and facing a decision of whether to transfer with the current law firm (which was merging with a larger one), or seek employment elsewhere. Just what I needed. Back at my desk, I sobbed at the insensitivity of my boss, and anger poured out to my coworkers. "If only he knew just how much energy I expend to organize my workload and concentrate on doing my best job. I try so hard not to entertain home problems during these work hours." My mistake was never having shared my thoughts and feelings with the boss, so he would spare another person such pain in the future.

My guess would be that my co-workers tired of my talking about Damian, but I didn't care. Not at all. I needed to talk about him. He was still a part of me. Though he was no longer physically on this planet, I had not let go of his presence in my life. Talking about him was like eating chocolate. It seemed good at the time and I enjoyed it, though it might not have been the best choice. Part of me felt as though I deserved the right to talk about him. After all, I was being punished for no action of mine. Besides, if you are traveling at 65 mph, can you come to an abrupt stop in a split second? Likewise, after almost 30 years of talking about him and us, I could not simply stop.

Within a few weeks, as my mind began adjusting to being a "widow," I mentioned Damian's name less frequently as it became easier to consciously refrain from mentioning him, as I no longer needed the crutch.

Dear Lord,
I ask you to let me be your instrument in guiding others toward an awareness of the need for sensitivity and understanding when working with a grieving person. At the same time, I ask for more patience with the people in my little corner of the world. They really do mean well. Amen.

My thoughts:

Widowhood

'Lord, Lord, King and Master of all things,
everything is subject to your power,
and there is no one who can withstand you
in your will to save Israel.

'Yes, you have made heaven and earth,
and all the marvels that are under heaven.
You are the Lord of all,
And there is none who can resist you, Lord.

—Esther 4:17a–17c

When I stood in my home after the undertaker left with my husband, thoughts raced randomly through my head like a race car nearing the finish line, unable to see what was being passed by. One of them was that I was now a "widow." Oh, what an awful word that was to me. I cringed whenever I heard it said. Words like *alone, lonely, black-clothed, cranky* and *old* came to mind as being synonymous with my new label. I was no longer a "Mrs." though I am still respectfully addressed in that manner. We took our marriage vows, "Till death do us part." He left this earth and our marriage was over. What a revelation! I still felt married. I still thought like a married person, but in an instant that position was stolen away from me.

It hurt. I was angry. I felt cheated. "Why did he have to leave me?" Just as there is no training manual for parents when a birth occurs, there was no training manual for handling my new status—widowhood.

Take your time. There is no rush. When you are ready—and if it is your desire—there are other widows in your community with whom you can socialize. It could be healing to share feelings with another widow—more to reassure yourself that what you are experiencing is *normal*. How to find other widows will be discussed more later. Perhaps rather than focusing on being a widow, a more positive status might be the label of being "single." There are many singles in the community who shop, work, dine, attend movies and concerts, or take continuing education classes alone. By joining singles groups and getting to know individuals in similar situations, you will have new people with whom to enjoy like interests. A church, volunteer organizations and political groups could be the nudge you need to get out and about, as well as introduce you to people with a common cause.

Dear Lord,
Please help me adjust to this new state of life—one that I prefer to call the "mature single." I need strength to try new things. I need courage to take the first steps. There is no doubt that with Your help, we will succeed. Amen.

My thoughts:

Invading His Privacy

Deep in water are the purposes in human harts,
the discerning man has only to draw them out.

—Proverbs 20:5

One of the most dreaded tasks after the funeral was going through my husband's belongings. It was his sacred space. He maintained his own sacred space, as I did mine. For more than 28 years I had never gone through his desk, wallet, dresser, end table or anything that was specifically his, without saying something first.

An eerie feeling filled me with guilt for touching those things after his death. I remember the long hesitation, nauseousness and trembling as I held his wallet, and removed each item to determine what to keep and what to shred. I wondered "What will I find? Will there be any surprises?" Whether by touching, reading or smelling each item, I was confirming that he no longer existed as a human being. As painful as this was, it was a healing task. And as I progressed, a stack of papers served as a reminder of agencies that I needed to be notify. His company ID and keys needed to be returned, his car insurance and driver's license had to be canceled and Social Security Administration needed to be informed that he had died.

Through sobs and globs of tears, I picked through items on Damian's desk. He had been corresponding with newly located cousins, all of whom were in the process of tracing their family ancestry. "How should I tell them?" I asked myself. On his desk I found jokes, religious items such as rosaries and prayer books, newspaper clippings and photos—all typical items for my husband to have saved. There must have been a half-dozen rosaries. Each had a special significance to him, but to others they would only serve as a remembrance of his devotion to praying the rosary. I gave them to our children. Fortunately, the only surprise I came across was some unexpected bills. For anyone who discovers unpleasant surprises, I would suggest trying to focus on the person you knew and loved. Second-guessing yourself over the "what probably was" and "why" serve no purpose but to torture the survivors, and that includes you.

Perhaps the biggest shock to me was what a pack rat my husband had been. He saved <u>everything</u>: saved candy wrappers, receipts, unopened junk mail. You name it; he kept it. Everything was stored in cardboard boxes—the kind that hold reams of copy paper. My children discovered about eight boxes, stuffed in the attic, which covered a decade. I parked my butt on the floor in front of the television and meticulously went through every item in each box—for weeks. Now only two 30-gallon plastic containers store the items I might need some day.

To look at Damian's clothing and possessions day in and day out was torture for me. It was like teasing that he might return. How unfair to me and the rest of our family to leave that impression of hope for us. I wondered how some people can wait months or years to empty their loved one's bedroom or closet.

While it was an unpleasant task, it was fitting to give the clothing to charity. People used to say that my husband would "give the shirt off his back" to anyone who needed it. My one dread was that I might one day see "that" shirt on a stranger. Once I recalled seeing a man wearing a shirt identical to one my husband had owned and I wondered if it had been Damian's. While there was a feeling of eeriness, I also experienced a reassurance that my husband would be pleased to have helped to clothe someone.

Damian's sacred space was no more. The task was completed and I was left with an empty feeling inside. The satisfaction came in the belief that I handled his possessions in a manner he would have pleased him. In so doing, I respected who he was in life when making the decisions to disburse them. Numerous people benefited from his having walked this earth and my adult children and grandchildren will have remembrances of this special man.

> Dear Lord,
> As I creep into the unknown areas of my loved one's personal items, I ask for courage, acceptance and understanding for whatever surprises there may be. Please shed the guilt I feel for trespassing where I would never go while my spouse was alive, as I know what I am doing is a necessary task. Amen.

My thoughts:

Forgive Your Spouse

'If your brother does something wrong, reprove him and, if he is sorry, forgive him. And if he wrongs you seven times a day and seven times comes back to you and says, "I am sorry," you must forgive him.'

—Luke 17:4

Strange, isn't it, how we hold onto stuff. For instance, a teenage girl treasures every gift, letter, corsage and love note she ever receives. That is until the day she gets angry with the then not so wonderful man in her life and burns or shreds everything he ever gave her. Then, instead of holding onto the "treasures," she may replace them with annoyances, disappointments, anger and hurts, which she grasps like possessions rather than letting go of them.

"How could you do this to me and to our kids?" I'd scream in the confines of my automobile. It simply did not make sense that if my husband truly loved us, he would allow himself to die without using every resource available to save his life. Now, of course, I was assuming this was the case. I most likely will never really know whether he did or did not seek medical attention or whether he actually suspected his heart was nearing its last beat. With the now strict confidentiality rules and laws concerning medical information, there is no possible way for me to determine these answers if I attempted to delve into them. My mind wasn't allowing me to think logically at that point in time. I was operating totally on emotion.

So now what am I to do with the anger, hurt, resentment, frustration and disappointment? Keeping it in was not helping me. It disrupted my sleep, prevented me from eating properly, and left me with a less than enthusiastic attitude toward life. I turned to some of my favorite authors for some answers. Louise L. Hay in *You Can Heal Your Life* encouraged me to ask myself, "Who do I need to forgive the most?" I had my answer.

What I did was write my husband a letter finally venting all my feelings, sobbing my heart out as I wrote. I wrote and wrote and wrote for hours. Then I let him know that I forgave him for leaving me and for all the past problems and

41

arguments we had for which I had held him responsible. Naturally, no one party is fully responsible for problems and arguments, so I asked for forgiveness for my part. In other words, I laid out my cards.

I wanted anger to release its grasp on my life. My anger was painful, both mentally and physically. By writing, I cleared the slate, as they say. I erased the negatives that had nourished my inability to get on with healing myself—to get on with my life. Simply by releasing my feelings with a pen and paper, my whole being was lightened. Almost immediately, I realized my posture was straighter, that I could take a deep cleansing breath with ease, that my appetite was returning and the pains in the sides of my neck disappeared. Most importantly, however, I noticed that my shoulders felt loose and somewhat lighter. The simple act of putting down my thoughts and feelings on paper eradicated the pent-up poison that was threatening harm to my body.

Forgiveness. Isn't that what Our Lord taught us by sending his Son on earth to teach us how to live? He gave us one example after another.

> Dear Lord,
> Thank you for the many people who have experienced tough times long before me, as they are able to share their experiences, learned truths, and guide me to find my answers. It helps me, Lord, simply to know that You are watching out for me. You are guiding me to hear Your answers. It is up to me to listen. Amen.

My thoughts:

Journaling

Wisdom brings up her own sons,
And cares for those who seek her.
Whoever loves her loves life,
Those who wait on her early will be filled with happiness.
Whoever holds her close will inherit honour,
And wherever he walks the Lord will bless him.

—Ecclesiasticus 4:12–14

When we were children, we kept diaries. I remember being about 12 years old when I received my first diary for Christmas. It had a lock and key, which meant I could write anything at all in it and as long as I maintained possession of the key, nobody could read what I wrote. This was powerful. Not only was I in total control of the diary, but also of what secrets I shared in its pages. Little did that child in me realize—nor did Santa Claus when he gave it to me—how significant a gift that would be.

My friends had diaries. We discussed their sizes, shapes, keys or keyless, and where we kept them hidden from *accidentally* being discovered. For my part, most of what I wrote in my diary was never shared with anyone. Little did I know that in actuality, I was listening to my inner self. The spirit within was dictating to me and I was hearing. The spirit within guided me through the teenage stages of life.

As an adult, I have found a new appreciation for the daily writing of thoughts, feelings, ideas, dreams, hopes, achievements and whatever else comes my way. Instead of writing in a diary that I can lock and hide, my *journals* are generally 5 by 8 in size, like this book, and have colorful floral covers. Most of them are lined to promote writing neatness.

Each of my half dozen journals is an adventure into daily living. When I want to see how far I have traveled in my life's journey, I pull out one and begin reading. By doing so, I remind myself of lessons learned, progress achieved, and then I can reevaluate goals and dreams. From deep within my being there is a wealth of wisdom and knowledge stored and ready to be drawn out. Some call it meditation; others call it prayer. Whichever name I give it, through the writing process, I connect with my inner self, my spiritual self. That self is released in my writing and offers wisdom to see the potentials that lie within awaiting discovery. So, what I thought was a clever way to keep secrets from my parents when I was a child really was the means of my growing spiritually using my own God-given resource.

Two books I recommend to learn more about the powerfulness of writing:

1. *Writing the Mind Alive—The Prioprioceptive Method for Finding Your Authentic Voice* by Linda Trichter Metcalf, Ph.D. and Tobin Simon, Ph.D. and published by Ballentine Books, 2002.

2. *LIFE! REFLECTIONS on your JOURNEY* by Louise L. Hay and published by Hay house, Inc. 1995.

At the time of a loved one's death and throughout the stages of healing, journaling can be a most precious and invaluable tool for direction and discovery. It also may offer answers to some of the puzzling questions that present themselves. This journaling time is magical. May you take advantage of your inner resources and the magical adventures those resources offer to you.

> Dear Lord,
> While I know you see me and listen to everything I say, as a human being, I seek your constant reminders that you will not abandon me. My brain tells me the truth, but I need reassurance. Through journaling, I am now aware that I will see You actively participating in my life if I tune into Your life in my body—my spirit—and listen to what You tell me. Thank you, Lord, for never giving up on me. I need You. Amen.

My thoughts:

Talk With Others

Blessed be the God and Father of our Lord Jesus Christ, a gentle Father and the God of all consolation, who comforts us in all our sorrows, so that we can offer others, in their sorrows, the consolation that we have received from God ourselves. Indeed, as the sufferings of Christ overflow to us, so, through Christ, does our consolation overflow. When we are made to suffer, it is for your consolation and salvation. When, instead, we are comforted, this should be a consolation to you, supporting you in patiently bearing the same sufferings as we bear. And our hope for you is confident, since we know that, sharing our sufferings, you will also share our consolations.

—2 Corinthians 11:3–7

In the Prayers of St. Francis we are taught that "it is in giving that we receive." Doesn't it make sense that to put ourselves out there to speak with others will help us?

As a young adult, I remember deciding one day to consciously speak to as many strangers as realistically possible. Not only was I going to speak to them, but offer them a smile indicating a positive message. You see, I had heard that if I gave a cheerful greeting to others that I would change that person's day and at the same time improve my mood.

During this experiment, I walked about two miles to work and spread my cheerful greeting along the way. Some people looked at me as if I were going to do them harm and their defensive mechanism produced a fearful energy as they hurriedly walked away. Others responded in a surprised manner, as if I had interrupted their stage of deep thought. Then there were those who simply gave a nod and didn't miss a beat in their haste to get to their destinations. Of all my "test" subjects, most fell into the second category, seemingly pleasantly surprised that a stranger would speak to them. That's kind of a sad commentary about society, at least in my area of the country. It would seem to me that we should be sharing greetings readily and returning them with the same enthusiasm.

Even though that experiment was several decades ago, I try to consciously notice and greet strangers today. And I know when someone does the same with me first, it just makes my day. Why? First of all, someone noticed that I existed. Secondly, that person sent positive energy in my direction.

Recently, while visiting Georgia, greetings and courtesies from complete strangers utterly overwhelmed me. Everywhere I went, such courtesies were commonplace. Even when I put on the directional indicating my desire to turn into another lane on the highway, I didn't have to wait for the opportunity to swing into the lane—instead, someone immediately waived to invite me to move in front of their car. The inner peace, happiness and a sense of pride in being human brightened my every day during that visit. Georgians proved the point I experimented with decades ago—being courteous is good for your soul and mine.

> Dear Lord,
> Remind me to think more of others and less of myself. If you were standing beside me, I'd offer to let you go ahead of me. Therefore, if I treat everyone as if they were You, Lord, I know that I would have a glow within my heart to keep me constantly uplifted. Amen.

My thoughts:

To Pick Up the Pieces or
Toss Them Out?

God is our shelter, our strength,
ever ready to help in time of trouble,
so we shall not be afraid when the earth gives way,
when mountains tumble into the depths of the sea,
and its waters roar and seethe,
the mountains tottering as it heaves.

—Psalm 46:1–3

After the funeral, life goes on. It felt as if mine had come to an abrupt halt. Eventually, I realized that there was nobody but me to pick up the pieces of my life and move on, or toss out some of the pieces to make a new life for myself. Either way, mine would be new in various aspects, depending upon the choices I make.

For instance, I chose to move out of the house we lived in for 16 years. I purchased a two-bedroom condo, which was perfect for me—no yard work, no outside maintenance—yet there were people nearby if I needed assistance or just needed to know others were there. Luckily, my 19-year-old son moved with me and remained for a year and a half. When he was ready to spread his wings, he asked if I would be okay if he moved out. At that moment I knew Damian and I had done something right by the fact that our son thought to ask before taking steps to make his move. This brought tears to my eyes. He was right. It was time for both of us to take the leap and get on with our individual lives.

Some widows I know chose to remain in their homestead. For me, the healing would have been a much longer process had I done that. While the same photos and trinkets adorn the walls of my condo, I do not live day after day reliving memories in the same rooms. Nor do I have to be in the room in which I found my husband's lifeless body. Instead, I relive a multitude of memories in my head—ones that take me to Washington, DC, Boston, Grand Rapids, Erie, New York City and Toronto, to picnics, family events, movies, etc.

Each person needs to do what feels comfortable and nobody can make those decisions—they belong to you.

I was told that I needed to forget the past in order to get on with my life. To those I now say, "Do you forget your parents and siblings, grandparents or pets when they die?" "Do you throw away their photos and memorabilia?" In my world, after such deaths, the survivors hang the photos and keep memorabilia on buffets, dressers, shelves or in special places. After all, it is the past that brought us to the present. It is that past that molded us into who we are today. And, that past is a treasure to preserve and hand down to the next generations. In the meantime, let that treasure serve as a healing tool.

The danger comes when we hold on to the past too tightly and attempt to live in the past. We must let go, like a mother needs to allow the umbilical cord to be cut to let her baby have a life of its own. So, too, we need to let go of the grip our past has on us to allow the birth of our new life. We are then free to nourish it to a healthy independent beginning.

Dear Lord,
When the pieces of my life feel like shattered glass, I desperately need You to hold my hand as I attempt to not only clean up the pieces but try to fit some of them together to make sense of my life. We can do it together. Amen.

My thoughts:

I Wish I Could...

Apply your heart to discipline,
and your ears to words that are wise.

—Proverbs 23:12

For years, I used to say "I wish I had time to..." and "someday I will..." After Damian died and all the busy work of moving and handling the matters related to his death were completed, I had many hours of unoccupied time. Because it was difficult to focus, ideas for constructive use of this time did not come to my mind. If I had had a Wish List of things I wished I had time to do, I would have utilized it for such tasks as to clean windows, repair torn window screens, cleaned the blinds.

Remember when you used to say, "I wish I could..." Perhaps now you can. If you have extra time to fill, pulling out that list of "I Wishes" could give you a variety of options from which to select. Included could be:

√ Windows to clean

√ Clothes to sort out and give away

√ Filing to do

√ Empty files of age-old "stuff" you don't need to keep

√ Collect shoes and slippers laying around the house, the garage, the basement, your car, and put them into one organized location

√ Sort loose socks

√ Organize and label photos

√ Make a list of the appliances and big items in your home, listing the serial number, brand, model, and, if you know it, the year purchased.

√ Photograph valuable items and put photos in safe deposit boxes in case of fire or theft

√ Repair torn window screens

√ Weed the yard

√ Sort items in attic and organize attic into sections in order to locate things easier

√ Write to those friends and relatives you keep saying you want to touch base with

√ Look up your family genealogy on the computer, or write to relatives to obtain details they can remember to help your search

√ Paint the closet that never got done

√ Remove and wash or dry clean the drapes/curtains

√ Clean the blinds

√ Put in closet organizers

√ Clean and organize kitchen cupboards

√ Wash the interior of the refrigerator

√ Clean the laundry room

√ Replace broken locks on doors and windows

√ Install more smoke and/or carbon monoxide alarms

√ Change smoke and/or carbon monoxide alarm batteries

√ Begin the story of your life for your children and grandchildren

√ Organize medical records, medicines, doctors, etc.

√ Organize assets, bank accounts, stocks, money markets, etc. into one place

√ Read those articles or books you've been putting aside

√ List things you want to get accomplished each day of an entire week, and check off the items when done

√ Research information you've been meaning to look up

√ Call long time friends you haven't heard from in awhile

√ List those with whom you would like to schedule a get together and add them to your list of things to do and get them scheduled on your calendar (they are probably procrastinating just like you)

√ Gather your cookbooks and list recipes you'd like to make

√ List groceries to buy from the recipes you're going to make

√ Watch a movie you bought but haven't taken time to enjoy

> Dear Lord,
> Would You whisper in my ear and remind me of all those things I always wished I had the time to do. During this period when time needs to be filled to keep me feeling human and needed, I ask your direction to select those tasks that are healing for me. Amen.

My thoughts:

Give Yourself Permission to Relax and Enjoy Living

Ask Yahweh for rain
at the time of the spring rains.
For it is Yahweh who sends the lightning
and gives the showers of rain;
he gives bread to man,
and grass to the cattle.
Because the seraphim utter futile words
and the diviners have lying visions
and publish empty dreams
and voice misleading nonsense,
naturally the people stray like sheep;
they wander because they have no shepherd.

—Zechariah 10:1, 2

With all of the things we must do after a spouse's death—settling the estate, perhaps maintaining a job and/or raising children, preparing meals, household duties—we forget to relax. Sometimes we simply do not remember what it is like to feel relaxed, as the daily stress of life and additional stress of world situations fuel our tension-filled lifestyle.

While there are a variety of choices you can make, may I suggest the following:

1. Read. Mark time on your daily calendar to put up your feet, sit in a comfortable place, and read a book of your liking, be it fiction, mystery, biography, love stories. Reading removes us from our problems and stresses. It puts us into another world—one where someone else guides our imagination to be free to visualize what the writer is describing. That break from the real world allows us to rejuvenate. It allows the tension to release from the neck and

shoulders. I suggest that at least an hour a day be devoted to this activity until your book is finished.

2. <u>Go to a Movie (or rent one)</u>. Plan to enjoy the entertainment of a movie at least once a week. The creative individuals who produced, directed, choreographed and performed in the movies enable you to simply get comfy and enjoy their vision of the book or script from which they worked. By giving yourself the gift of watching a movie, you take your mind off of your current life situations. Through the movie you may even come up with ideas or solutions to some of your problems. Other problems may become trivial. Regardless, depending upon whether your selection is a suspense thriller, love story, fantasy or action flick, your enjoyment may lift you up and put you into a better frame of mind in which to continue your daily journey.

3. <u>Listen to Music</u>. The most relaxing and joyous part of your day could be listening to your favorite music. Your selection may vary with your mood, the weather, the environment and any number of variables. Music tends to calm the nerves and opens our reception to healing thoughts, ideas and words.

4. <u>Crafts</u>. Should you enjoy crafts, this would be an excellent time to pour yourself into your craft of choice—from knitting and crocheting to quilting, ceramics, stained glass making and sewing. To do so could give your mind a vacation from the day-to-day tasks. You may be surprised not only with the quantity you can produce, but also with the quality and originality of your masterpieces.

5. <u>Take a Vacation</u>.

   a. Before you eliminate this selection from your list, it doesn't have to mean an expensive getaway. It could be taking the time off from work and having a daily agenda to do things you never have the opportunity to do. This could be spending a day at the beach—sunbathing, swimming or relaxing in a lawn chair. This would be a day to get back in touch with nature and to hear your inner voice, which is so easily blocked out by everyday commotion.

   b. Locate the best means of transportation to visit a friend or relative, who will not only allow you to enjoy the pleasure of visiting with their family household, but who will also give you space to relax and get in touch with your inner self—perhaps even your inner child.

6. Treat Yourself to a Theater Performance. Whether alone or with friends or relatives, this removes you from daily reality and probably gives some humor to the sometimes-mundane things we do.

> Dear Lord,
> In my small box that I feel I am squeezed into, I tend to forget the tremendous number of choices that are available to me. Perhaps you could walk me past fliers, newspapers, posters or run commercials that shout their messages and show me the opportunities inviting me to have fun. Amen.

My thoughts:

Friends Come And Go

By his command he sends the snow,
  he speeds the lightning as he orders.
In the same way, his treasuries open
  and the clouds fly out like birds.
In his great might he banks up the clouds,
  and shivers them into fragments of hail.
At sight of him the mountains rock,
  at the roar of his thunder the earth writhes in labour.
At his will the south wind blows,
  or the storm from the north and the whirlwind.
He sprinkles snow like birds alighting,
  it comes down like locusts settling.
The eye marvels at the beauty of its whiteness,
  and the mind is amazed at its falling.

—Ecclesiasticus 43:14–20

Throughout our life I believe that God moves us like pawns on a chessboard. We get placed in a position where certain people influence and/or teach us things we need to learn to advance in life. We, too, are put in places to affect and teach or help others.

As with my childhood friends, most of whom are no longer in my life, my husband was placed in it for a reason. What the Lord's reason was, I may never know. For one thing, Damian taught me to laugh and helped me find my sense of humor. Having been a perfectionist and bearing much responsibility in my family, laughter did not fit in very well during my growing up years. After my husband came along, through his joking, teasing and antics, he made me laugh. I didn't realize that I had a sense of humor. Actually, I thought I was born without one. This was a gift my husband gave to me—a discovery I may have eventually made on my own, or then again, maybe not.

My husband was my very best friend ever. We shared our past joys and hurts, our future dreams, our likes and dislikes. He was like a girlfriend in that he listened to what I had to say, and acknowledged it. Even as the years passed and we were married for more than 25 years, we would still find joy in dining together—either in silence or a mixture of silence and conversation. We enjoyed common interests, such as pipe organ concerts, plays, miniature golf, bowling and even playing bingo.

When friends disappear from our lives, sometimes we wonder why; sometimes we know why. Their absence generally leaves a void. Memories remain as long as we wish to recall them. Those memories keep those friends alive in our hearts to continue learning from the relationships, to remind us of our lessons learned and our discoveries. Memories are gifts to treasure.

When I step back and review the possible reasons for my having been placed in my husband's life, I guess my role was to teach him how to receive love and how to give love. Part of that receiving and giving was through the births of our five children. A child's unconditional love is so pure and as close to a heavenly experience as we can probably have on earth. Another reason for my being in his life may have been to help him discover a sense of purpose. This sense of purpose was to help others in a wide variety of ways using his many talents.

Other childhood friends remained in my life for a couple of decades then drifted away only to surface again a couple decades later. Often we are able to pick up where we left off and fill in the blanks with ease. For me, such has been the case since my husband's death. Those friends who knew me so very well have been able to be a source of strength and trust, a foundation that was built so many years ago.

Security is such an important part of life. Those long-time friends with whom we shared life's joys and sorrows, slumber parties and the Ouiji Board also witnessed and experienced the cruelties of other children as they name-called and tormented us. We also received the sacraments of the Roman Catholic faith together at a time when our individual personalities were evolving. These friends are those we hold a lifelong trust to be there for us and us for them.

Dinners and gatherings with those friends aided me in returning to my old self and rediscovering the strengths and confidence I once had. It isn't so much what they said or did, but simply being with them and reminiscing together that put me in a place of accepting those former aspects of self and reclaiming them.

Are my friends aware of the influence they have on my life? I doubt it. Just as I am unaware of what ways I may be an influence on them. Perhaps one day we will share this information.

Dear Lord,

Help me to be the kind of friend that I would like someone to be to me. Oh, how I know the importance of being a good friend, especially now when I need one to just sit with me in silence or to gently ask me leave my corner of the world and venture outside of my comfort zone. Amen.

My thoughts:

Waves and Flood of Grief

I want you to be happy, always happy in the Lord; I repeat, what I want is your happiness. Let your tolerance be evident to everyone; the Lord is very near. There is no need to worry; but if there is anything you need, pray for it, asking God for it with prayer and thanksgiving, and that peace of God, which is so much greater than we can understand, will guard your hearts and your thoughts, in Christ Jesus. Finally, brothers, fill your minds with everything that is true, everything that is noble, everything that is good and pure, everything that we love and honour, and everything that can be thought virtuous or worthy of praise. Keep doing all the things that you learnt from them and have been taught by me and have heard or seen that I do. Then the God of peace will be with you.

—Philippians 4:4–9

Just as water symbolizes cleansing, tears release built-up anger, tension, frustration and hurt. So often we hear others say they "held back the tears" and for a short period of time that can be proper. However, crying is good and healthy. To hold back the tears and not allow the body to release and cleanse is to store the negativity within, which in turn may contribute to the development of diseases, such as cancer, in the future.

The waves of flood of grief hit me hardest when driving alone. It could be a song that was playing like "I'll Be Home for Christmas" that opened the floodgate for me as well as thoughts of conversations that took place during the workday. Passing by a favorite restaurant or a random thought could be the unexpected trigger that set off the grief.

You will experience waves of grief that overcome you like an unannounced storm. They can creep up at the most unexpected places and often-inopportune times. And, just when you think you have passed through the phase of mourning, a wave of grief overtakes the acceptance you felt you had achieved.

Take a wound after surgery. It may weep excess fluid for awhile before it heals completely. Perhaps the incision heals quickly in some areas and takes longer in others. How the body heals is a mystery. The body has its own healing capabilities. We need to trust our bodies to let us know how best to assist it in doing its work.

Your body may tell you to get more sleep—so as to ward off infections; eat fruits and vegetables for extra B-vitamins; drink more fluid to replace that excreted through stress and tears. Love and take care of yourself.

> Dear Lord,
> Your Mother showed us how to grieve with faith and trust. Please give me that faith and trust in my days of hurting and loneliness. Amen.

My thoughts:

Why Am I So Exhausted?

Do not abandon yourself to sorrow,
do not torment yourself with brooding.
Gladness of heart is life to a man,
joy is what gives him length of days.
Beguile your cares, console your heart,
chase sorrow far away;
For sorrow has been the ruin of many,
and is no use to anybody.
Jealousy and anger shorten your days,
and worry brings premature old age.
A genial heart makes a good trencherman,
One who benefits from his food.

—Ecclesiasticus 30:21–27

Most weekends when an invitation was extended to join family members, I would tell my adult children and my mother that I had to finish housework and laundry. After awhile, I began to feel guilty about making that same excuse to them week after week, but I knew if I didn't take the time to do the work, it would still be there on Monday.

Then one day, while I was vacuuming and wiping the dripping sweat from my eyes, it dawned on me. I am the only one doing all of the housework and laundry now. What a revelation! Yes, I knew it. I had made the statement, but it had not sunk in until now. How could it take almost a year for this realization to hit? How stupid I felt that it took me so long. After all, I went from having four others at home chipping in to just me. The change occurred all within a year, and it was no wonder that I was exhausted.

My new project was to concentrate on how to best organize myself and my time to accomplish more with fewer steps so that I could accept my family's invitations. For example, I began to organize my closet by grouping my work clothes on one side, separated by slacks, blouses and dresses and non-work clothes on the other side, also separated into slacks, shirts, sweaters. Then, when I placed my hung laundry in the closet, I automatically sorted them into the appropriate areas. Now, when I get dressed in the morning, I'm not looking through everything several times or running down to the laundry room to find that red blouse I know I washed. (I should have figured this out many years ago!)

Another example of saving energy was to make a list of all errands that needed to be done and, if possible, accomplish them in one trip. So, armed with a grocery list and coupons, and the list of places I needed to stop, I'd plan where to go first and make a big circle from my home and back again. Maybe I'd leave home and stop to get gas, get a prescription from the drug store, return a video, get a present from a gift store, buy groceries, and then return home. It was amazing how much time was saved, not to mention the gasoline. How simple it sounds now.

Another discovery was that I could stop after work to get groceries, or whatever the errand, by taking a different route home. It is amazing how programmed we get and just don't think to make a simple change. I had to chuckle when it became apparent that my reason for hurrying directly home to make dinner no longer made sense. My husband had been diabetic and had to eat at a specific time to maintain his regular eating habits and blood sugar. Once I recognized I had no reason to be home and to eat dinner at a specific time, I became more flexible.

Six months after moving into my condo, I reassessed the placement of items my home. It was incredible how I was wasting space. Things I did not use or need but took up space got moved to the basement, tossed out or put in a part of the storage area for a future garage sale. Then, I rearranged furniture and knick-knacks to be more practical and pleasing to me.

I found that by keeping a "To Do List," things did not get forgotten. As they were accomplished, I crossed them off the list. At times, I maintained two such lists—one for tomorrow and one for general reminders for upcoming tasks.

There are so many ways to lessen our burdens. We need to slow down, sit back and evaluate. The time and energy we save by doing this simple task can leave us with hours of free time to enjoy whatever we choose.

Dear Lord,
Please give me strength to accomplish the necessary day-to-day tasks. Perhaps I need to reconsider my living situation. Maybe I need a smaller place to maintain more easily. Remind me that there are alternatives as simple as sorting out choices that are available, and selecting the one or two that would serve me best. Amen.

My thoughts:

Finding My Special Gift

There are a variety of gifts but always the same Spirit; there are all sorts of
service to be done, but always the same Lord; working on all sorts of different
ways in different people, it is the same God who is working in all of them.
The particular way in which the Spirit is given to each person is for a good
purpose. One may have the gift of preaching with wisdom given him by the
Spirit; another may have the gift of preaching instruction given him by the
same Spirit; and another the gift of faith given by the same Spirit; another
again the gift of healing, through this one Spirit; one, the power of miracles;
another, prophecy; another the gift of recognizing spirits; another the gift of
tongues and another the ability to interpret them. All these are the work of
one and the same Spirit, who distributes different gifts to different people
just as he chooses.

—1 Corinthians 12:4–11

Here I am faced with limitless free time, which I don't want to waste. I realize
how precious time is but what do I want to do with it? What are all the things I
always wished that I had the time to learn or time to do for others? What is the
instrument I wanted to play? Did I want to act? What about volunteering?

The Lord says we each have a special gift from Him. Have I identified the gift
He gave to me? For me, my dream has always been to create artistic pieces and to
write books. As a child, raised by parents who lived through the Great Depression, the thought of someone writing or being an artist meant that person would
never earn real money. My dreams were squelched.

When I was unable to locate the type of inspirational book for widows, that
provided some guidance and said, "What you're feeling is O.K.," I decided it was
time for me to begin my writing career. This is the initial fulfillment of my
dreams and, I believe, by doing so, I am using a special gift that God gave to me.

In clearing space physically and in my head, the words flow easily. Feelings
give a vibrancy to my voice that hopefully conveys a useful tool from which oth-

ers will benefit. My voice comes from being tuned in to my spiritual self. That spiritual self connects with the universe and the Lord and draws from its energetic field the insight to be shared.

While we all cannot be writers or artists, perhaps your gift is to run marathons, lift weights, prepare gourmet dishes or write computer programs. Perhaps you always wanted to skydive, get a college degree or travel to Europe or Australia, South America or Iceland.

I cringe when I hear someone say "I don't have any special gifts or talents." I don't believe that. What I do believe is that that person has not cleared the space around him or her to discover it. By clearing the space, I mean to find an uncluttered area to be completely still—no television, no radio, no children, no animals or other people. It is a place of total silence. If it is impossible to have a totally quiet space, you could go into a room, close the door and play some very soft, slow, meditation music. Take a couple of deep breaths and sit or lay comfortably while listening to your breath. Then close your eyes. Ask your God, "What are my talents? What special gifts have you given to me?" Continue to breathe slowly and wait for your answers.

If your answers do not surface with your first attempt, try again—on a daily basis, if possible. To get in touch with your spiritual self takes practice and patience. Once you begin hearing your answers, it will be such an inspiration that you may use this as a tool on a regular basis for the clarity it will bring to your life.

Dear Lord,
I trust You to give me the patience and drive to seek the answers that You want me to hear. My life has been congested and does not leave room to hear what You are trying to tell me. I am ready, Lord. I need to discover deeper levels of myself through Your love. Thank you, Lord. Amen.

My thoughts:

Obsessive Behavior

The heart knows its own grief best,
nor can a stranger share its joy.

—Proverbs 14:10

For 20 months, I fought an almost uncontrollable urge to shop. Consciously, I was aware that I should not be spending the money, but the force was stronger than my control. What was I buying? New drapes, bedding, a camera, computer, computer desk and things for our children and grandchildren.

Did I attempt to think about WHY I was shopping? Yes. But my mind went blank. So, I asked myself some more questions about my compulsion:

☐ Was it to punish or get back at Damian for leaving me? No, I didn't feel that was the answer.

☐ Was it to camouflage his memories? No, not that I was aware of.

☐ Did I deserve these things? In a way, I did. After all, I felt like everything was taken away from me the day he died. Shopping was like stuffing myself with chocolate ice cream or M&M's until I didn't feel very good.

☐ Did shopping make me feel better? Yes and no. Yes, when I was in the store, it felt absolutely freeing and wonderful to buy whatever I wanted. No, when I got home and realized the amount of money I spent.

The rationalizing that we do is amazing! There were no longer children at home. Therefore, there was no need to sacrifice my needs and/or wants for their necessities. I had sacrificed for almost 30 years. Now, I could spoil myself with gifts. After all, my husband was no longer bringing me home surprises, so I had to surprise myself.

After almost two years of this kind of rationalizing and questioning my objectives and feelings, I was pleased to discover an answer for my shopping compulsion: When I purchased items to treat myself or to make others happy (which resulted in my gratification), I fulfilled my emotional needs. It made me feel loved and cared about, as strange as it may sound. With this discovery, I not only was able to reign in my spending habits but I had to be more disciplined in my purchases. Did I really need to have the items I tossed into the cart? Did my grandchildren really need another toy when their moms were stuffing bags of toys to give away? Did they really need a third winter coat?

In addition, there was nobody to remind me of upcoming annual or twice yearly bills that I needed to be prepared to pay (car insurance, license renewal, car registration, etc.). Would I be able to make these payments? What about emergency expenses? Would I be prepared should the need arise for a new furnace, stove, refrigerator, water heater, or a car batters? Reality had struck.

Loneliness made me feel like I deserved something to make me happy. The possessions were supposed to fulfill that need. Right? But they were not doing the trick. I needed to find another way to satisfy my needs.

Dear Lord,
When I am out of control, I would appreciate a mirror to show me what I am doing. It is in recognizing unwise choices that I am able to make better choices. Please awaken me to those choices. Amen.

My thoughts:

Look Alikes

"So, I say to you: Ask, and it will be given to you; search, and you will find; knock, and the door will be opened to you. For the one who asks always receives; the one who searches always finds; the one who knocks will always have the door opened to him."

—Luke 11:9–11

You are walking down the street and come face to face with "someone" who looks just like your recently deceased partner, but you know it can't be because he died. It is an eerie sensation. The first time this happened, I was parked at a traffic light and turned to my left. There in the car next to me the lookalike sat staring straight ahead. Pound. Pound. Pound. My heart raced. Then almost as rapidly, my heart rate dropped. Of course it wasn't him.

Until now, you most likely never put much thought into why it is that after someone you love dies, you seem to see so many people who look like that loved one.

A counselor friend of mine says that the lookalike I saw and maybe you have seen *is* our loved one taking on that person to let us know his presence is still real in spirit. It was not a comfortable concept for me until I thought about it for awhile.

Even today, when I see one of my husband's lookalikes, I stop in my tracks and whisper "Thank you, Damian." I acknowledge his gift to me.

Dear Lord,
When I see someone who reminds me of my spouse, I know it is You letting me know that my spouse is watching out for me; that I am not alone; that You are providing healing comfort for me. The same is true if I hear a song that my spouse enjoyed or sang, or the smell of a cologne my spouse wore. I appreciate the good feelings these bring to me if only for a few minutes. Amen.

My thoughts:

Thank You, Lord, for My Faith

The apostles said to the Lord, 'Increase our faith.' The Lord replied, 'Were your faith the size of a mustard seed you could say to this mulberry tree, 'Be uprooted and planted in the sea,' and it would obey you.

—Luke 17:5, 6

If a widow does not have faith, I do not know how she gets through widowhood. Without my faith, I would have had great difficulty pulling myself from the depths of depression. My belief lifted my inner spirit with faith that the Lord, through the Holy Spirit, was with me every step of the way. For some reason unknown to me, my God decided that my husband's purpose on this planet was completed.

Just as faith helped us repeatedly throughout our marriage, I rely on it now in this journey alone. I remember when my husband was out of work for a year. There were times when we did not have money for bread and milk for our children for the next day. As hard as I tried to believe that the Lord would provide for us, my human side worried. Lo and behold, a letter would arrive from a family friend who sent us a check to take the family out to dinner. Little did that friend know that check provided us with enough food for a week. Another time when we reached the same desperate situation, a couple of large cartons of food were sent over by a church we did not even attend, as someone had turned in our name for food donations. I can still see the whites of our children's eyes as they quickly emptied the boxes to see what wonderful items were there to be shared.

That Christmas we had an abundance of love, gratitude and thankfulness for the kindnesses of many who were not thinking just of themselves and their families that holiday season. I doubt that any of my adult children will ever forget that winter. We were blanketed with God's wondrous love. With each week my worry lessened as we witnessed our survival. Even our pediatricians waived fees when we took our children in for sick visits and they gave us medicines. It was a humbling experience, kind of like the Lord Jesus being born in a manger. Call it a miracle, human kindness, God's intervention or synchronicity; God's love was obvious to our family.

For those with faith in the Almighty God, these would be answers to prayers, which can manifest themselves in numerous ways. Perhaps, by someone bringing food or striking up a conversation with a stranger that ends up leading to a job, or reading a note posted on the bulletin board at the local laundry that puts you in touch with an agent for your proposed book. Being aware of opportunities and synchronicities are gifts from the Lord. For those of faith, these gifts enable us to continue on our path and better our lives.

As you read this, perhaps numerous sayings come to mind:

• The Lord won't give you more than you can handle.

• The Lord giveth and the Lord taketh.

Perhaps you will recall a time when you were thinking of a friend, the phone rang and that friend greeted you! Or maybe a time when you forgot your lunch money but found a couple dollars on the ground on your way to work. Or, just as you were leaving for work, the telephone rang and it was a wrong number; but you later realize that by answering that call you missed being in a serious automobile accident. These are times of synchronicity or divine intervention. When these special surprises present themselves to me, I offer a prayer of thanks.

> Dear Lord,
> Again, thank you, Lord, for my faith. I appreciate this special gift You have given to me more now than perhaps ever before. Paired with faith is trust, and I place my trust in Your hands—to open my heart to Your love, to open my ears to hear You talking to me, and to open my mouth to be a human voice for Your message. Amen.

My thoughts:

Laughter in the Home

Glad heart means happy face,
where the heart is sad the spirit is broken.

—Proverbs 15:13

Like eating a cream puff and believing there were only a couple of calories in it, that is what laughter is like in the home. It makes light of heavy worries. It lessens heavy loads. It feels really good. The only big difference is that there are NO calories in laughter, and the exercise itself may even make you burn a few calories.

I know you may not feel like laughing at this very moment. The timing may need to be just right. Thinking about it may open up the opportunity for some light moments to enter into your world, which could lead to a moment or more of laughter.

Recalling some of the craziest things you ever did, such as a tremendously fun party you threw or attended, a surprise you pulled off for someone or the most humorous comedian you ever listened to may be all you need to stimulate the brain to think about humor.

When I tried this on myself, I recalled a long van ride with our five teenagers. We were traveling across New York state. They were tired and bored and we were not pleased about listening to the complaints. Quietly my husband slipped a Bill Cosby tape into the player. Before long we were all laughing so deeply that tissues were being passed right and left to wipe the tears. Cosby's stories of his family's experiences hit home, but his had a twist of humor that we never thought to add into our stories. He made life seem silly, and had quick comebacks that made sense as they diffused tough situations. That was probably over a dozen years ago, but it was one day that we all still pull out of our pocket of memories to share when we get together. It brought us together like handing out our favorite chocolates, and comforted us in the memory of a fun time together.

When I need a laugh, that is my favorite memory to recall. It doesn't cost a cent for the entertainment it provides.

Dear Lord,

As I remember the wonderful times when laughter filled us with the greatest feelings of love and joyfulness, may those times fill me with those same feelings as I relive them in my memories. Those memories are gifts to treasure forever, and to pull out whenever I so choose. Thank you, Lord. Amen.

My thoughts:

Why?

Jesus went on from there and reached the shores of the Sea of Galilee, and he went up into the hills. He sat there, and large crowds came to him bringing the lame, the crippled, the blind, the dumb and many others; these they put down at his feet, and he cured them. The crowds were astonished to see the dumb speaking, the cripples whole again, the lame walking and the blind with their sight, and they praised the God of Israel.

—Matthew: 15:29–31

Over and over, I wondered, "Why??" Why did my husband die? Why didn't I see it coming? Why didn't I…? Why? Why? Why?

For the most part, we don't obtain the answers to our questions. It just is. "When it is your time; it is your time." This was one of Damian's favorite expressions. The Lord must have simply decided that my husband's work on earth was done, and He wanted Damian for his next assignment.

The "Whys" are draining on us. They pull us down into a negative area. They really serve no healing purpose as far as I can see.

The "Whys" lead to the guilts. The guilts lead to depression and perhaps anger and hurt. It doesn't make sense to focus on negative energy.

So, why am I focusing on the Whys? To encourage you not to.

Instead, I tried to focus on how grateful I was. It was then that a warmer, comfortable feeling filled my being. It kept me in an upbeat spirit, remembering the good times and the qualities I enjoyed in my husband. It reminded me of how much I was loved. What a wonderful gift that love was and is, as I know my husband will love me forever. And I will love him forever.

Why did the Lord guide my husband and me toward finding one another? He must have had it in His plan, and He knew we would make the best of our time together.

Dear Lord,
I do know better than to question why you took my spouse to be with you. Being human, Lord, I sometimes cannot help but revert to childishness and ask "why?" Please know, Lord, that I love You and really mean to thank you for the years that I did have with my spouse. Thank you for the gift of my spouse in my life. Amen.

My thoughts:

Listening

He who turns his ear away from listening to the Law,
his prayer is an abomination.

—Proverbs 28:9

Did you ever notice the difference in what you hear when you are alone beside a body of water? In that time of solitude, the sounds of nature shout their praises. Leaves crackle in the wind and the wind blowing between a tree's leaves and limbs has its own distinctive sound. Water ripples and fish jump in the water. Numerous birds take flight and gently land, communicating with one another along the way. These are sounds we do not hear unless we listen to the silence.

During our busy lives of working—whether at home or in a workplace—raising families, caring for sick family members and the like, we frequently do not make the time to listen.

An awareness of ourselves develops as we fine-tune our listening skills. Your inner voice speaks and can be heard because it is not being blocked by other noises. It may remind you of how fortunate you are to have had the marriage, with all of its joys and woes, and treasure the memories that can never be taken away. My inner voice lets me know when I should contact someone who needs to hear from me. That person may be feeling depressed, lonely or have a problem troubling them and he or she may need some reassurance.

Listening to my inner voice leaves me with a calmness, a peacefulness and a trust that the Lord is guiding and taking care of me. He simply asks that I open my ears and heart and listen to the messages He is constantly sending to me.

The messages cannot be rushed. If I am anxious to hear what I am to do next, often it is my thinking that I hear and not my inner voice. I need to allow myself to relax and silence my mind. It is a skill that may take some work, but it is well worth the effort.

Listening also means hearing what others are really saying. Perhaps a friend is telling you about a problem she is dealing with. You hear her story. With your listening heart and mind you recognize that she does not see the actual problem. By listening and blocking out what is going on in your life, you are able to focus on what that person is really saying. Your inner voice tells you how best to approach the subject and lead that person to discover the real problem.

I realize how infrequently we take the time to truly listen and hear—whether it be to ourselves or to others. We need to focus on learning the skill of blocking out other thoughts and ideas, and fine tune the ability to zoom in on the actual problem or solution, whichever the case may be.

By developing my listening skill, I am letting go of my need to control situations. This control is released to the hands of the Lord. As much as I try to control a situation, it is in His hands. He will allow us to make decisions, but the ultimate control is out of our hands. Once I realize this fact, I release my need to control and let the Lord know that I am turning my life over to Him and will trust his loving guidance.

> Dear Lord,
> "Ephrata" is a word spoken by your followers centuries ago. I, too, wish to listen better—especially to what You are trying to tell me. Please keep my ears open to hear You speak and offer your guidance. Amen.

My thoughts:

Those Irritating Rubber Bands

I can hear a voice I no longer recognise,
'It was I who relieved your shoulder of the burden,
your hands could drop the labourer's basket;
you called in your trouble, so I rescued you.'

—Psalm 81:6, 7

When thinking back over our years together, at first I remembered the happiest times. As months passed, in crept the little irritations I had with things Damian said. You would tend to believe that those irritations would be long over and done. Well, just hold that thought, as I tell you a story.

After living in my condo for almost three years, I decided that the way I originally arranged my closets just was not convenient. During a Saturday afternoon, while emptying out the closets, I found a couple of rubber bands strewn about the carpet. Where did they come from? I guessed I must have dropped them, though I did not recall seeing any. I picked them up and put them in my desk organizer tray where I store rubber bands. As I continued my cleaning and rearranging, I found a couple more rubber bands on the carpet. A wee bit irritated and puzzled, I picked them up and tossed them away. This happened a few times. I was too busy determining what should be placed where to put much thought into the rubber bands. The last step of my project was to vacuum both closets and my bedroom. I put away the vacuum cleaner, returned to the bedroom and, you guessed it—there were two more rubber bands on the carpet.

I burst out laughing. There was absolutely no way anything I did could have caused those rubber bands to be there. At that moment I knew it was my husband making his presence known to me. So I acknowledged him.

"Okay, Damian, I know you are here and are having some fun with me. Thank you." I didn't know what else to do, but it made logical sense to affirm his being there with me.

Later, I phoned one of my daughters and relayed my story.

"Mom, you should have known it was Dad. You know how he used rubber bands and collected them." (We had a player piano and he always wanted an abundance of rubber bands to have on hand to wrap around the piano rolls when another one snapped.)

Yes, I had forgotten. He used to become annoyed if we threw one out, scolding, "You don't know when you might need it." He would wrap them around a paper clip holder or stuff them into a specific drawer. This seemed peculiar to me, but as they say, "to each his own."

The end of the story: I haven't seen another errant rubber band since.

When our loved ones want to reach us after their passing, they find ways to do so. If we don't pick up on their clues, they try and try again until we get the message. This is something my children and I have discovered these past six years.

I recommend the books *Heaven and Earth—Making the Psychic Connection,* published by Simon and Schuster Source, 2001, by James Van Praagh and *The Other Side And Back—A Psychic's Guide to our World and Beyond* published by A Dutton Book, 1999, by Sylvia Browne to further comprehend how spirits, who have passed on, communicate with us. These books are enlightening. Now when I recognize Damian's presence, I welcome him and feel comforted.

Dear Lord,
Thank you for the humorous ways in which our loved ones can let their personalities come through to us. I appreciate these light moments. We are fortunate to have such a means of communication with our loved ones who have moved on to life with You. Thank you, Lord. Amen.

My thoughts:

Were You Really As Happy As You Remember?

God rises to shouts of acclamation,
Yahweh rises to a blast of trumpets,
let the music sound for our God, let it sound,
let the music sound for our King, let it sound!

God is king of the whole world;
play your best in his honour!

—Psalm 47:5–7

When you think back over the years of your marriage, you tend to see all the wonderful, happy times you now miss. At least for me, initially, I viewed my marriage through rose-colored glasses. I felt it would be unfair to my spouse to think badly about any aspect of our married life—even if it had nothing to do with marriage in itself.

There is no doubt that we had numerous memorably happy occasions. However, every day was not a celebration.

As I take an honest step backward into my memories, there were days when I felt totally alone—even though there were seven people living in our house. It seemed that everyone was busy, each in his or her own life, and I was doing the expected tasks of a mother, wife, daughter. Some days it seemed that I didn't have the time to take care of my needs—or that I didn't have the money to do or buy things for me.

As wives, mothers, sisters, daughters, you are raised to give—and if you are of certain religious affiliations, you feel guilty if you want. Therefore there can be a void. This sense of being worthless, if conveyed to another, could appear to be self-pity. Which brings you around to believing that your main role is that of being the caregiver.

This is when you realize that the age in which you were raised groomed you to sacrifice your needs for those of others. Yet, when you recognize this sacrificing, you were acting like martyr. There was no way to reach a win-win situation.

Fortunately, times have changed. Society now allows for an adult female to care for herself and recognizes that she can give more of herself to others if she is well cared for.

No, times were not always happy, but look at the growth that has transpired over the years. Now can be the time to use that growth to work for you. Now is the time to find that happiness—how to define it and how to achieve it.

Dear Lord,
Life is so very complicated. There is no book that tells us what is right, what is close to being right, and what is definitely wrong. You are the only one who knows what my life has encompassed. I am grateful for Your constant love, even when I did not make the best possible decisions for others or for me. Thank you for your love. Please continue to help me make the discoveries necessary to achieve my happiness. Amen.

My thoughts:

Our Hidden Inner Strengths

Neither to son nor wife, brother nor friend,
*   give power over yourself during your own lifetime.*
And do not give your property to anyone else,
*   in case you regret it and have to ask for it back.*
As long as you live and there is breath in your body,
*   do not yield power over yourself to anyone;*
since it is better for your children to be your suppliants,
*   than for you to have to look to the generosity of your sons.*
In all you do to be the master,
*   and do not spoil the honour that is rightly yours.*
The day your life draws to a close,
When death is approaching, is the time to distribute your
*   inheritance.*

—Ecclesiasticus 33:20–24

We all have those women in our lives for whom we have tremendous respect, and, yes at times, envy. Whether we know them personally or not, their strengths and outstanding characteristics are magnetic. Drawn to observe such women, we silently wish we could have their admirable qualities.

Then, amidst conversations with others, someone remarks that you have leadership qualities and that person respects your organizational skills. While to you, it seems that such skills are nothing unusual. You may wonder, don't we all have those skills and talents? It is an awakening to discover that what comes naturally to you may not come naturally to me.

While with a group of my close friends, we had such a discussion. In turn, we each stated the traits we admired in each other. Collectively, we were astonished to learn what strengths we presented to others. Hidden from us were gifts we did not recognize in ourselves. Thanks to the openness of our honest friends, we departed with a sense of greater self-esteem.

Think about a compliment you may have paid to someone. Were they surprised? Were you taken back by their reaction to your compliment? As humans, it seems we tend to put ourselves down. We are too hard on ourselves and tend not to recognize our talents and skills. It may be worthwhile for you to have such a discussion with a trusted person, to have a mirror image of what they see in you. The strengths identified for you could then be specific areas for you utilize in appropriate areas of your life. Perhaps this could lead to a new career.

Dear Lord:
It would be a blessing for you to put others in my life to mirror my strengths for me to recognize. Not only am I grateful to You for all that I am, for those you put in my life, but for the vast possibilities of success that are ahead of me. Please give me the tools to recognize the talents I have so I can better serve my brothers and sisters. Amen.

My thoughts:

Allow Dreams to Form a Bridge

He who listens closely to the word shall find happiness;
he who puts his trust in Yahweh is blessed.

—Proverbs 16:20

Some of my children and grandchildren began having dreams about their father and grandfather. I was jealous because I was not a recipient of such dreams. About four months later, I had one. Nothing in the dream made any sense to me. The people didn't belong together, as they were from different parts of my life, but that didn't matter to me. What did matter was that I was able to spend some time with my husband. Damian looked wonderful; he laughed, and we had a grand time. For the entire next day, I was on such a high.

After I told a counselor about the dream, she said that spirits find it easiest to communicate initially with their loved ones by intercepting dreams. She said that it takes a tremendous amount of effort for a spirit to use their energy in this manner. With the spirit being so new to that life, they haven't learned how to use their powers yet. Even for spirits, practice is required.

Everyone is, of course, welcome to their own beliefs and interpretations when it comes to dreams and spirits. For me, I choose to believe. It is comforting to believe that Damian is now a spirit in heaven. What a comfort it has been to feel that he is watching over our family, guiding us and that he still loves us. Whether this is absolute truth or not, I really do not care. It makes me feel safe, warm, comfortable and loved.

Since the first dream, I have had many more. One occurred on a day when I was recovering from sinus and bronchial infections. Even though I was sick, I went to work. That day, the other support staff person did not show up so I was left assisting a number of attorneys. By the end of the day I felt like a dishrag with a brain to match. Tears welled up in my eyes as I used total concentration to keep them from dotting my face—until I left the building. Then they let loose, and for my 10-minute walk to my car, they flowed freely. I was late leaving the office so I didn't run into anyone I knew and very few people remained downtown. Even

101

so, I don't think I would have cared. I had the right to mourn if I felt it. And mourn I did.

"I wonder if he will come to me in a dream tonight?"

Yes, he did. It was very weird to be conscious in a dream, at least that is how I perceived it. During the dream, it suddenly occurred to me that I was having the dream, that Damian was in it, and he was firmly hugging me in a very protective and gentle manner. Okay, so it was a dream. I didn't want it to end. When I awoke and remembered it, I realized that I must have been so relaxed and comfortable that I fell into a deep sleep after understanding what was happening. It was wonderful.

If you haven't had a dream of your loved one, you may want to give some thought to your beliefs about dreams. Before you go to sleep, speak to your loved one. Tell him or her what you would like. It is my understanding that spirits have no concept of time as we know it, so answers may not be provided in a timely manner.

Sweet dreams.

Dear Lord,
My dreams can be a puzzle to me. Sometimes they are scary; other times they are soothing. When my loved one presents himself in a dream, often when I recognize him, he disappears. This saddens me. I look forward to seeing my deceased family, friends and spouse in my dreams as they bring love and comfort. Please let them know that I thank them for their efforts to present themselves to me. Thank you, Lord, for the gift of their appearances to me. Amen.

My thoughts:

There is No Rush

And when you pray, do not imitate the hypocrites: they love to say their prayers standing up in the synagogues and at the street corners for people to see them. I tell you solemnly, they have had their reward. But when you pray, go to your private room and, when you have shut your door, pray to your Father who is in that secret place, and your Father who sees all that is done in secret will reward you.

—Matthew 6:5,6

Whether you celebrate birthdays, holidays, anniversaries or other special occasion with your family and friends the first year is totally up to you. The good intentioned may strongly urge you to join them. However, only you know how you feel, and, more importantly, how much celebrating you can bear to be around. It is not selfish—it is self-preservation. Those who truly love you will understand and accept your judgment.

Because my husband died on December 7th, that first Christmas was a blur. When someone talks about it and after I listen to them, some of the day comes back to me, but very little. There was no joy, no celebrating and while there was no doubt love, it was overshadowed by the painful memories and realization that I would never again celebrate Christmas with my husband. Our tradition was history. There was no special intimate dinner celebration; no carefully picked out simple gift.

This reality manifested itself repeatedly throughout the year especially on his birthday, my birthday, our anniversary and then the birthdays of our children. The first year was the worst. Over time, by telling stories of past years and joining in laughter, often mixed with tears, our souls were cleansed. My husband was then present in a different way—a healing way. Even the youngest members of our family delighted in reminiscing.

Unlike widows of decades ago who wore black for an entire year and were shunned should they go out socially during that period of mourning, this is the 21st century and none of that fits our current attitude. What you do and when you do it is totally your decision. Emily Post is no longer here to give us etiquette advice.

There is no rush to get back into the swing of things. First, you need to determine what kind of swing that will be. Perhaps you will need a safety swing with a bar to hold onto and keep you from falling off until you get used to the experience. Or maybe you will feel gutsy and go for the big swing and fly high. No doubt you will watch to see what others are doing. You may feel insecure or silly. But if you recall words of wisdom spoken to you when you were young, you may "put on a happy face" and wing it. That happy face may just trigger some small degree of inner happiness to let you soar.

The bottom line is you can set your own time line for future events. Whether you entertain the suggestions of others is up to you. Unless a counselor, clergy member or another widow is guiding you, most likely the person advising you has no idea how you feel or grieve or hurt.

There is also a danger in getting back into the swing of life too slowly, mourning too long, and wallowing in self-pity. Take for example, the woman whose husband died four years ago. She visits his grave weekly and she cries herself to sleep nightly. Most likely this description brings to mind someone from your past, whom you would not wish on anyone.

In your healing plan, may the Lord guide you into making the best decisions concerning when and how to return to daily activities and celebrations.

> Dear Lord,
> Please keep the Holy Spirit by my side, to whisper in my ear and guide my choices. You are well aware of pain. The pain You endured for us. The pain you endured due to the less-than-best decisions made by your disciples. I trust You through the Holy Spirit to protect me and my loved ones, to open my heart and ears to hearing and feeling your love. Thank you, Lord Jesus, for caring about me. I need You. Amen.

My thoughts:

Power of Prayer

God is our shelter, our strength,
ever ready to help in time of trouble,
so we shall not be afraid when the earth gives way,
when mountains tumble into the depths of the sea,
and its waters roar and seethe,
the mountains tottering as it heaves.

—Psalm 46:1–3

At the time my husband died, the "whys" and the "if onlys" filled my being, as I'm sure they did to you. I believe my prayer was as basic as being the act of breathing in and out. Initially, To breathe took all of my energy and concentration. Never before had I realized just how laborious breathing could be, and that very action was my simplest form of prayer.

How could I not believe in a Higher Power when I saw so many people who were touched by the death of my husband? How could I not believe as I saw my young adult children stand before a packed church and share testimonials about their father? How could I not believe as friends came to our home and took over thinking for me so I could just be and grieve? Your experience may be somewhat different, but evidence of the Higher Power will be there.

With the passage of time, the working of the Higher Power in my life was etched in the path that I took. For me, it was completion of a college program and obtaining a paralegal certification; learning that some jobs that pay more aren't always worth the stress that comes with them; battling cancer, and winning; moving into a safe and economically efficient condo; losing my job only to find myself and gain strength; almost losing my son to a dissected aortic aneurysm and pulmonary embolism (like that from which actor John Ritter died); landing a job with caring people and doing work that I very much enjoy; and having the ability to cut the cords and give my blessing as two adult children moved hundreds of miles away. The Lord's hand has been involved in every step of this journey, and I have recognized Him.

Furthermore, in watching the progressive healing process in each of my adult children, and witnessing their helping each other is further testimonial to the Lord's working in my family's life. As you shed the anger, fear, perhaps even hate, and open yourself to the Lord's grace, you too will witness his working in your life.

> Dear Lord,
> When I close my eyes and offer my words of praise to You, I am thanking You for cradling me and my family in your endless love. This is my prayer—that those who read my words will feel your loving hands holding theirs and guiding them to live the best possible life in a fulfilling and meaningful manner. Amen.

My thoughts:

Allow Yourself to be Outrageous

Kindly words are a honeycomb,
sweet to the taste, wholesome to the body.

—Proverbs 16:24

After four or five years of being widowed, why not consider actually enjoying life a little. Okay, so you would like to, but what are your options? Look around. What are other women doing that you may consider interesting? Lo and behold, you identify an intriguing pasttime, then "the buts" set in: But I don't have the talent. But I don't have the right kind of clothes. But I am not as outgoing.

My gosh, I wondered to myself, am I going to sit in my condo and vegetate for my remaining years watching soaps, endless real time shows and old movies that I've seen several times? No. There is more to life than that—and more to life than babysitting grandchildren. It is my time to have fun, to be useful and to make a difference in the lives of others. But how?

First, I joined some women friends who so were enthralled with the "*Secrets of the Ya Ya Sisterhood*" movie that they formed a group called the "Ya Ya's". We, as the ladies did in the movie, designed our own hats at one member's home. She had a table set out with beads, feathers, lace, ribbons and a glue gun. One member took a white baseball cap and glued on feathers, lace and pearls. Another added ribbons and birds onto a straw hat. Some hats were truly outrageous, and others were truly gorgeous.

Naturally, everyone had to have an outfit to go with their hat. One friend, Tess, wore a straight black sleeveless evening dress with a black boa and long dangling earrings. Her dress still had the attached original price tag from 15 years ago—like Minnie Pearl. Leanna wore a mumu. Some wore decorated jeans. When we get together, it is a "whatever floats your boat" event. We each bring a dish to pass, sit around and tell hilarious stories. To date, we have not gathered enough nerve to wear our outfits in public. However, we do gather as the "Ya Ya's" in traditional clothing and go to movies or dinner together. Laughter is a must for any of our gatherings.

This fun occurs whenever we get together. Sometimes we alternate meeting at each other's homes. We each have "Ya Ya" names like Short Woman With Big Dreams (in charge of clothes), Princess of All Seasons, Dream Catcher (in charge of dreams), Tassel Tosser, Smokin' Mama and Shady Lady.

Another Ya Ya, Elizabeth, was elected to be our "sexatary," who takes the "minutes," so to speak, at each "meeting" and reads them at our next gathering. As you can imagine, there is much hooting, howling and tear-streaked cheeks as we enjoy being outrageous.

A nationally organized group is the Red Hat Society. Started in 1985, the Red Hat Society has local chapters with 20 or fewer women. The women all must wear red hats and gloves and purple dresses and they go out in public in their outrageous attire to dinner, movies, benefits and whatever else their members decide to do. Women under the age of 50 are invited to join as "Pink Hatters," who wear pink and lavender. For information go to www.redhatsociety.com. When I shop for clothes I see that most women's clothing shops and/or departments have an area dedicated to this organization's requisite color combinations. You may be interested in checking out the Society's web site to see what groups are in your area.

Such gatherings, which some would consider to be outrageous, bring out the inner child in us, stir up our juices for having fun and give us the permission to play and make believe, as well as to do nice things for others. We don't need such a group to do the latter, but it adds to the festivity of it all. There is also a sense of belonging, of not being alone or lonely.

Perhaps these ideas do not suit you, so why not consider joining an acting group—like a community theater—and hone your speaking and acting skills. Discover the you that has not had the opportunity to blossom and grow. If you are not comfortable with acting, perhaps marketing, stage, costumes or office work are areas in which you might consider volunteering.

Maybe you used to clown around, or always wished you could act like one. Well, you can. Clowns can do silly things, nice things and look ridiculous. They make people happy. Seeing smiles on the faces of others would be completely heartwarming. Check your yellow pages or the Internet to make the connection you need.

Local newspapers regularly list community activities. Select a couple to investigate. Make a list of your questions before placing a call for information so you don't miss anything. Remember to block out the "buts" and don't let them creep in and discourage your decision-making or risk-taking efforts. This is especially true if negative aspects about yourself have ruled your decisions in the past. This is a new start for you. As you may have been told throughout life, "You can do anything you want to do if you put your mind to it."

> Dear Lord,
> Please fill me with confidence and love. After all, if I have confidence and love, I can do anything I set out to do. May the love satisfy the need of another one of your children through my actions or words. Thank you for the gifts you have bestowed upon me. Amen.

My thoughts:

Lending a Helping Hand
or Ear to Others

There was a lawyer who, to disconcert him, stood up and said to him, 'Master, what must I do to inherit eternal life?' He said to him, 'What is written in the Law? What do you read there?' He replied, 'You must love the Lord your God with all your heart, with all your soul, with all your strength, and with all your mind, and your neighbour as yourself.' 'You have answered right,' said Jesus, 'Do this and life is yours.'

—Luke 10:25–28

Well-known bereavement author Elizabeth Kubler-Ross identified and labeled "Reaching Out" as the sixth and last stage of the grief process.

Throughout my life, I have been instructed to be apostolic, meaning to follow the example of Jesus' apostles, who went out teaching about Jesus and living the kind of life He preached. So it is a natural evolution of the bereavement road I've been on to feel a calling to minister to other widows.

When my husband died, I was surprised that my widow friends did not rush over to be with me and support my children and me. Of all people, they knew what we were going through. On the other hand, having now experienced the death of a spouse of almost 30 years, I too, can understand how difficult it may have been for them to be around us—to relive their experiences again through us.

After attending a Beginning Experience Weekend, which is a type of Christian retreat at which speakers share their divorce, widow or separation experiences and lead participants' reflection and small group sharing activities, I knew I wanted to become active in the Beginning Experience ministry. I felt so blessed to have a team of total strangers who gave up not only a full weekend for me (and my fellow participants), but also spent many hours in preparation for that training. This team of men and women purchased tons of food and prepared nutritious and plentiful meals for us. Others came on Friday to greet us, carry in our luggage and help us to feel at home.

At my weekend, the only widows there were two women (who made presentations) and one who assisted in the kitchen. But I was not teamed up with any of them. These sensitive women realized my need to identify with them and each took me aside for a little time to talk. I was touched and very grateful.

Fortunate for me, I was asked to attend the orientation and evaluation to determine whether I was ready to undertake this mission. I say fortunate for me, because as we minister to others, we are ministering to ourselves, too.

As you heal and discover your new identity, you too may find yourself thinking, at first, about ways you can spread your apostolic wings to others. Perhaps, at first, you will feel the need to be a better listener. Maybe you will find that you are more patient and understanding of others. You may recognize that a friend cannot afford a babysitter to get away for a few hours and you could offer to babysit. Or a friend may need help with home repairs and can't afford a professional and you have the skills to offer.

Please remember to love yourself. Remember that God loves you unconditionally and He is always with us. If we allow ourselves to rest in total silence and be open to His message, He will come to us.

We have passed through grief to acceptance, from suffering, death, resurrection, and now on to mission. Sounds to me like we have journeyed the road Jesus walked a couple of millenniums ago.

Recently a work friend was at home watching a video. Her husband chose to go to their bedroom to watch TV and phone his cousin. While talking with his cousin, he suffered a heart attack and died. He was in his early 50s and his wife is 40. What a tremendous shock to this family, who had just celebrated their youngest daughter's 17th birthday the night before.

This friend didn't return to work for three weeks. When I saw her at the funeral, she said she was fine, but she functioned like a robot doing as she was expected. Her spirit was not there—it was dormant.

A few days after she returned to work, I spoke with her. Having forgotten that I was a widow until I reminded her, and not knowing another widow to speak with, she was eager to retell her story. My heart melted as she lit up and was so happy to have me listen to her experiences. "Was that normal?" she'd ask after recalling her feelings of expecting him to return and wondering if she could have done anything to save his life. While listening to my friend's story I relived mine but to know that I was making a difference and helping her to heal and move on was worth the pain. We are all learning constantly on this journey of life.

Whatever your religious affiliation, it's your turn to lend a helping hand or ear to others.

Dear Lord,
Even though it is painful to listen to talk about the death of a spouse, I know that by doing so helps not only the person speaking but me, too. By reliving our story, we are making the fact that it occurred become real to us. At the same time, it is our attempt to put some closure on the death. Please help us to recognize that it is through dying that we join you in eternal life. It is this eternal life that is our ultimate goal. I need to be reminded of this. I need to be reminded that eternal life is unlike anything we can imagine as a human being. Thank you, Lord. Amen.

My thoughts:

Transitioning

He who lives forever created all the universe.
The Lord alone will be found righteous.
He has given no one the power to proclaim his works,
and who can fathom his magnificent deeds?
Who can assess his magnificent strength,
and who can go further and tell of his mercies?
Nothing can be added to them, nothing subtracted,
it is impossible to fathom the marvels of the Lord.
When a man finishes he is only beginning,
and when he stops he is as puzzled as ever.

—Ecclesiasticus 18:1–7

Throughout our marriage, my perfectionism gradually shifted to indifference to many things. The extreme shift was not beneficial to anyone. In losing my identity, I lost my strength, my willingness to grow and the drive to follow my instincts. As I look back, I see that I surrendered my identity to my husband and lost the will to fight for it.

Whether this alteration of my expectations was due to his strong will or my weakness, it is unclear. However, I do not believe it was a deliberate change. Through time, life events, circumstances, deaths and hurts, I lost my strong will. My guess would be that the transition that occurred within me affected my husband's life too. Whether it was negative or positive, I will never know.

Interestingly, losing my identity was such a gradual transition that it went unrecognized by me. When or how it began, I am not sure. Can I blame anyone? No. I would take full responsibility for not being aware of what was happening to my life. Looking back, I can only imagine that this transition would have made life more difficult for my husband. For as I cared less and less about what I believed in, it left more for him to manage.

Why am I sharing this aspect of my marriage? Through the many readings, review of talk shows and conversations with others, I am aware that this is not unusual. It is like a silent illness that strikes and affects everyone in a household. In today's modern age, we are so overly busy with family, work, perhaps school and community events that we squeeze out time needed to reflect on our lives objectively.

Becoming aware of such transitioning in your life, you can be instrumental in suggesting that it could be happening in a loved one's life when you see it happening. Whether that loved one realizes it or not, you have been a good friend in planting the seed to be nourished and grow at a later time.

As for me, my partner has passed and I am left to recreate my life in as positive a way as possible, enabling me to be both productive and available to assist others. It is a time when I can be true to me; to be honest in my undertakings and in rejecting events that are of no interest. In so doing, I am setting an example for my adult children and grandchildren to do likewise, as long as my choices are not offensive or hurtful to others.

After all, don't we go through transitions/phases throughout our lives? Now we can recognize them as we reach a new one, and have some say in how it will evolve.

Dear Lord,
Transition is what life is all about. We are progressing like a newborn evolving into a toddler, a toddler evolving into a preschooler, and so forth. As we listen to the elderly, it appears that the evolving continues to the day of death. Thank you, Lord, for this ongoing growth process of reaching You. Amen.

My thoughts:

Can I Love Again?

'So I say to you: Ask, and it will be given to you; search, and you will find; knock, and the door will be opened to you. For the one who asks always receives; the one who searches always finds; the one who knocks will always have the door opened to him.

—Luke 11:9, 10

More than three decades have passed since I was single. As I see my widowed and divorced friends find a special love, I begin to ponder that to have a man in my life would be quite nice. However, even after four years of being alone, I do not feel the necessity to find another husband. After all, it has taken almost four years to get comfortable with my new life. I have even reached the point where I enjoy living alone and I can actually say, "I am happy."

"Can I love again?" Today, I believe I could answer "Yes." Whether I could or would get married again would depend on the man, his priorities, and how compatible we were. It is very difficult to imagine being married to another man. I believe that we would have to be friends and companions for awhile first before making that decision.

Back in my dating days, a woman never asked out a man. That was the man's role. The perfect gentleman would open a car door and help the lady into her seat, then close the door for her. He would open the door for a woman and he would pause at a doorway to let a woman walk through first. "Dating" meant to go with a gentleman to a movie, out to dinner or some other type of entertainment. A woman or man could date numerous individuals. "Going steady" meant a couple dated each other exclusively.

Today, the rules have changed. Either a man or a woman can extend an invitation to attend a movie, a dinner or a party. If a couple is "dating" or "seeing" each other, they are not going out with anybody else. Nobody "goes steady" anymore. The niceties of old, related to car door and doorways, rarely happen.

If you have male friends from church or some organization to which you both belong, you may feel comfortable chatting with them in groups. Perhaps you have even had opportunities to have informal, one-on-one discussions. The more you can speak with men informally in non-judgmental, comfortable situations, the easier it becomes. By speaking honestly with one another about subjects such as being alone, divorced, separated or widowed, you learn more about how men think. This is especially important for those of us who were married to one man for decades.

Perhaps the simplest way for a widow to ease into dating again is to double date with a friend or relative. This way, I can see it being less intimidating, with others around and lack of conversation would be unlikely. You could have a great time. Another idea would be to "practice" asking a man out on a date by inviting a friend out to dinner or a movie with you. For me, this would be a male friend who I am confident would like the same restaurants or movies. Once you ask and he goes out with you, it gets easier to ask him or another friend the next time. No, your friend does not need to know you are "practicing" your techniques on him, but there probably is no reason not to tell him either. He could give you hints on how to do it better.

I invited such a friend over to dinner. We had known each other for more than three years through our involvement a peer grief support group for people who are divorced, widowed and separated. Even though I had known him for a long time, I was very nervous. My insecurities surfaced, but I chose to ignore them and think positively. As it turned out, we had plenty to talk about. We both had a delightful time and have alternated hosting dinners for each other. This gentleman has a girlfriend and they invited me to join them in attending a local high school play. Awkward? Yes, indeed. But my choices were: Do I stay at home and watch TV or read a book or do I go with friends to a play? I chose to attend the play. We had together dinner first, went to the play, and I was brought home afterward. I learned from this experience that to turn down an invitation because of my insecurity would have left me feeling lonely and always wondering how the evening would have turned out. Now I know.

My adult children talk about setting me up with gentleman they know. My insecurities resurface, and I share my fear that he will not like me. You know how the "buts" and "what ifs" creep in. Again, I have a choice whether to consider them or shut them out. My children remind me that he will feel just as insecure. From talks with my other male friends, I have to agree with them.

At this stage of my life, I am open to whatever opportunities for enjoyment come before me. I trust my wisdom and pray to the Holy Spirit to guide my life and to determine which individuals would enhance my life—maybe even become that new love. And I trust the Holy Spirit will do the same for you.

Dear Lord,
I am so alone. Nobody likes to be alone. While I know that you are always with me, and I see evidence of your presence in my life, please open my eyes. When you send special men into my life for me to choose from, please help me to recognize that they are gifts from you. Thank you, dear Lord.

My thoughts:

When Am I Ready to Risk Dating?

He alone performs great marvels,
his love is everlasting!
His wisdom made the heavens,
his love is everlasting!
He set the earth on the waters,
his love is everlasting!

—Psalm 136:4–6

There is no magic answer to when you are ready to start dating. You leave yourself open to being vulnerable. You look around and see others who may have married on the rebound and struggle in their relationship. Since dating could lead to a serious relationship, you need to answer "Am I ready to become involved with another man?" What should you do?

It wasn't until I'd been a widow for five years that I felt an interest in having a gentleman with whom to dine, attend a movie or the theater or simply for conversation. I had written a goodbye letter to my husband, thereby closing that chapter of my life and I was ready to begin the next chapter. There lingered in me a yearning to have someone to care about me, to hug me, to need me and I felt that man needed to sweep me off my feet. Since I do not enjoy hanging out in bars or drinking alcohol, what were my other choices? I had already been involved in community activities and had not met anyone of significant interest.

A couple of my single friends mentioned online dating. The more we discussed this manner of meeting a compatible gentleman, the more it peaked my interest. It made sense that by getting to know the thoughts and desires of an individual and becoming friends first, a basic relationship could be formed. I joined a well-known online dating service and shortly thereafter had several online male friends. We corresponded for months when eventually most went by the wayside. Through online dating I learned that many men are just as nervous about meeting women as we are about meeting them. After the three-month trial period ended, I joined another popular online dating service.

125

It was at the second dating service that I met and bonded with my male friend, whom I am now dating. We mutually agree that by putting our cards on the table, we were able to ask and answer questions of each other, safely give opinions, and grew in friendship first before we exchanged addresses and phone numbers.

This may not be the comfortable way for you to seek a male companion to date. You may prefer the traditional way of meeting him through blind dates arranged by friends and relatives, through meeting at organizations or church or by chance meeting, say in a grocery store or on a bus. Whatever the means you prefer, using discretion is a must and let a relative or close friend know who you are meeting, where and when, as a precaution.

Once you create the profile of the type of person you seek, it would make sense to determine where this type of person might be found. Perhaps you will determine that you need to become more active in your church, join a charitable organization, cultural organization, social group, club, or even a dating service, be it local or online. Speaking with friends and relatives about the qualities you seek in a date may result in your being introduced to a friend, relative or coworker of one of them.

As with other situations in which you had to make decisions, prayer, research, self-searching are all tools available to help. It would seem that you need to determine the what qualities you won't settle for less than. What behaviors will you not tolerate? Do you want another person's child to raise? Do you want another man to raise your child? Do you want to have more children of your own? Granted you are simply beginning to date but these are questions for which you need answers in order to make the best choices for you.

Some women write down the specifics they want in a man: physical attributes, education, career, family-orientation, religion, nationality, age, etc. There is belief that once these qualities have been identified, the energy force draws like a magnet and brings that person into your life. I prefer to believe that the Lord answers my prayers. Whatever the belief, it is worth the time to focus on whom you are seeking to serve as your companion.

Perhaps the most important aspect of preparing for dating is to know yourself. What are your expectations? What are you prepared to offer in a relationship? How fast do you want to move in a relationship? What are the reasons you want a date? Are you seeking a companion or a life partner?

After considering these questions and many more, perhaps you will be ready to answer the question, "When am I ready to risk dating?"

Dear Lord,
You know that I don't want to live alone for the remaining days and years of my life. To think of dating again is intimidating. Please give me the confidence to date; give me the open mind to see the best person for me and not react merely to emotions. Thank you, Lord, for guiding and watching out for me. Amen.

My thoughts:

Regular Doctor Visits

Better a poor man healthy and fit
than a rich man tormented in body.
Health and strength are better than any gold,
a robust body than untold wealth.
No riches can outweigh bodily health,
no enjoyment surpass a cheerful heart.
Better death than a wretched life,
and everlasting rest than chronic illness.

—Ecclesiasticus 30:14–17

While I am not in the medical field, may I suggest that for at least the five years after the death of your spouse, you get regular medical checkups—both with your primary care physician and your gynecologist.

My intention is not to alarm you, but to keep you alert to what your body may be telling you. The body is a miraculous creation. It tells us what it needs we have to be in tune to being aware of what it is telling us.

The majority of women I know who are widows have developed some form of female cancer within the first five years of widowhood. It could be a coincidence, but because I have seen this happen more in my widowed friends than in those who are married, I have to wonder if the turmoil that our bodies undertake during those first few years feeds the cancer.

For myself, I was about 3 1/2 years into widowhood when my body let me know that something was seriously wrong. I kept envisioning a baseball-sized circle in my abdomen, but didn't have a clue as to what this meant. I would wonder if I had a tumor, but of course dismissed it, as it was a condition I certainly did not wish to entertain. These visions would occur randomly and during the same couple of months I was feeling ill. My primary care physician sent me for testing to determine the cause of diarrhea that wouldn't stop. Results were normal. At the same time, I started having two menstrual periods a month for two months (and I had been post-menopausal for more than a decade). A biopsy showed pre-

129

cancerous cells—several stages. My surgeon explained that there are four stages of pre-cancer before the cells turn cancerous. The recommendation was that I have a complete hysterectomy to remove all of these cells to avoid cancer.

Needless to say, this was traumatic. My support, confidant and best friend was not there to help me make this life-altering decision. I felt terribly alone, not to mention terrified. Which would harm me more, the surgery or not having it? The time had come for me to be strong and take action.

I purchased a book on the subject, did research on hysterectomies and spoke with other women who had been in this situation. My research, faith in the Lord and prayers led me to agree to the surgery.

Would you believe, my surgery was on 9/11/02, the first anniversary of the terrorist attacks. Life and surgery goes on; I totally turned to the Lord to guide the surgeons and nurses, and I accepted what was to be. Fortunately, I came through surgery quite well. My family and friends were extremely supportive. I am fortunate. They were there for me every step of the way and throughout the two months of recovery.

The autopsy of the removed organs showed that I had first stage cancer, which confirmed for me that my decision had been the right one. Every three months for two years I get checked to make sure I remain cancer free.

Following surgery, there were concerns: hormone therapy or not. It was another decision I faced. I visited the library and read up on my options; I spoke with my primary care physician and my gynecologist, then made the decision that I felt was best for me. Just as every person is different, so is every person's final decision.

> Dear Lord,
> I have some serious thinking to do and major research of my own to under-take. Please hear my heartfelt prayer asking that you clear my brain to process the information necessary for me to make an informed decision. Please guide me to select the best information to read. Lastly, please give me patience to slow down, relax and listen to what my body is telling me through your Holy Spirit. Lord, I am most grateful to You for constantly being with me and for me. Amen.

My thoughts:

It Has Been My Life Long Dream to...

'I am the bread of life.
He who comes to me will never be hungry;
he who believes in me will never thirst.
But, as I have told you,
you can see me and still you do not believe.
All that the Father gives me will come to me,
and whoever comes to me
I shall not turn him away;
because I have come from heaven,
not to do my own will,
but to do the will of the one who sent me.'

—John 6:35–39

Perhaps you always wanted to fly an airplane. Or take a vacation to Europe, South America, Australia, Africa or Alaska. Maybe you wanted to write a book, go parachuting or sailing, visit relatives you have never met or decorate your home in a nontraditional way. What better time is there than now to do what you always dreamed about but never had an opportunity to try.

What will others think? Does it really matter what they will think? They have their own lifelong dreams. Events in life keep us from fulfilling our dreams. If you have an opportunity and the means to fulfill those dreams, this may be your only chance. Do you want it to pass you by? Maybe taking some time to journal on the subject will give you some insight as to your choices.

Now, if you are newly widowed, I would not recommend you chase your dream just yet. You need to give yourself three or four years to adjust to all the changes. You have people who care about you and may be very worried if you do something totally out of character during the first couple of years of widowhood.

Once your life has become normalized, then it would be time to think about making your dream come true. Following your dream does not mean escaping from the reality of dealing with issues that must be faced and dealt with. Those things must be accomplished first. Then you will be ready to open your heart and enjoy new adventures.

For example, if you never worked and your financial situation leaves you with no choice but to enter the workforce, then that would be your immediate concern. Once you have received the necessary training, started your job and have a new routine in place, then would be the time to consider your next challenge. Meanwhile, there is no reason why you couldn't begin a "Dream List" and collect brochures and information for future use.

Since sixth grader, my goal has been to write a book. For a number of reasons, I didn't have the opportunity to attend college. This left me believing that I didn't have the ability to "write". Then, at the age of 52, after enrolling in college and graduating with Paralegal Certification, my dream of becoming a writer resurfaced. It was as vivid as when I was 12 years old. However, it was my journals that I wrote after my husband's death that gave me the inspiration to develop this book. At times it was not easy to ignore the negatives that would sneak in from past tapes that played in my head. If I had not tuned them out, you would not be reading *Amending Dreams*.

We've all heard, "The sky is the limit." I don't see an end to the sky, do you? I don't see a hindrance to achieving anything I put my mind to doing, unless my mind says, "No, you can't." If my mind gives me that message, then I must still be playing old tapes from many years ago—words that were spoken to me as a child. It must be time to change the tapes to messages that give me permission to try and not to give up easily. Whoever said "You can achieve anything you put your mind to" certainly knew what they were talking about. If you believe in positive energy, chi, the Holy Spirit, greater power, or whatever name you call this source of supernatural energy, draw on it to reach the goals you set for yourself. You go girl; you can do it.

> Dear Lord,
> We know you have given us more tools that we are even aware of to attain our greatest capacity to achieve success in a number of ways. We are fortunate to have Your love to present itself in people and ways that produce positive effects. Thank You, Lord.

My thoughts:

Amending Your Dreams

Now Joseph had a dream, and he repeated it to his brothers. 'Listen' he said 'to this dream I have had. We were binding sheaves in the countryside; and my sheaf, it seemed, rose up and stood upright; then I saw your sheaves gather round and bow to my sheaf.' 'So you want to be king over us.' His brothers retorted 'or to lord it over us?' And they hated him still more, on account of his dreams and of what he said. He had another dream which he told to his brothers. 'Look, I have had another dream' he said, 'I thought I saw the sun, the moon and eleven stars, bowing to me.' He told his father and brothers, and his father scolded him. 'A fine dream to have!' he said to him. 'Are all of us then, myself, your mother and your brothers, to come and bow to the ground before you?' His brothers were jealous of him, but his father kept the thing in mind.

—Genesis 37:5–11

I recall walking around—you know that nervous energy that I'm talking about—and feeling that my dreams were totally shattered. *Our* dreams no longer existed. Nobody asked my permission to steal those dreams away from me. After all, there were almost 30 years of work to create, plan, and emotionally await their fruition that was invested in those dreams. Gone. Totally disintegrated. "It is not fair!" I would shout in the solitude of my home.

Through much effort, self-reflection, counseling and speaking with others, I am at a point where I have begun amending dreams. Instead of the vacations *we* had envisioned, I am planning vacations to locations new to me. Some are with family; some are with friends. What is amazing to me is the fact that I can even contemplate planning a trip with a group—like the Auto Club or another organization where I know nobody. This might be only a day trip, but it is a start.

We had planned to purchase an RV and travel to various locations around the country. In the amended dream, the thought of relocating to a warmer climate is settling in my brain. The enjoyment is in the research of my choices—any possible locations my heart desires to investigate! I realize that I am not tied to where I reside or to my current occupation. With my work skills I can send resumes anywhere in the country. I need to trust myself and the Lord to make the best possible decision.

When I was a child, I used to spend many summer hours at our next door neighbor's home putting together puzzles with the grandfather. I recall the patience and perseverance it took to find at difficult piece that was crucial to completing a section of the puzzle.

Currently, I am working on a giant puzzle as I begin preparing for retirement. I know where most of the pieces will fit, but there remain some that have not been turned over yet. Those are the missing pieces that have yet to be identified and properly placed. Pieces of this puzzle could be changed from time to time, and I allow for that flexibility.

My spiritual connection with my husband leaves no doubt in my mind that he will be with me and continue to help in whatever way he can to make the best of my life. He would not want me to grieve endlessly, nor would he want me to live like a hermit. I highly doubt that your husband would either.

At the end of this book are some pages that I hope you will use to jot down ideas for amending your dreams. Not that you need to work on them at this moment, but simply write down words or phrases that come to mind that you can contemplate at a later time. Such notes may trigger other ideas to surface during your workday, while shopping, watching television or the like.

The toughest part is beginning the thought process for amending dreams. It is also giving myself the permission to make such changes. The rest simply falls into place once we give it momentum. After all, our dreams are not gone—they are being amended. Happy amending!

Dear Lord,

I ask that you open my mind to new opportunities and places that have not been even slightly considered in my lifetime, which could be of interest and benefit to me. I know that you will guide and protect me throughout any and all decision-making processes that I may choose. Thank you for enriching my world. Thank you for the ability to choose. Thank you for this fabulous earth you created. Amen.

My thoughts:

Permission to Dance Again

Do not abandon yourself to sorrow,
  do not torment yourself with brooding.
Gladness of heart is life to a man,
  joy is what gives him length of days.
Beguile your cares, console your heart,
  chase sorrow far away;
for sorrow has been the ruin of many,
  and is no use to anybody.
Jealousy and anger shorten your days,
  and worry brings premature old age.
A genial heart makes a good treacherman,
  one who benefits from his food.

—Ecclesiasticus 30:21–27

Congratulations! Though you could probably, and may have, added many additional chapters to this book, it is my hope that by now you possess balanced energy; life as you knew it has blended with the new life you are creating; that the joys and sorrows each have their own place, and you have taken the time to discover your unrealized talents, strong points and desires. Now, you are ready to incorporate them into your daily life.

A renewed happiness has awakened and stirs within, and it is ready to take off and send you dancing. Whether you enjoy the waltz, macarena, salsa maringé, hip hop, cultural, twist, cha cha, or other reggae, there are a variety of exercise studios, dance studios and clubs to suit your fancy.

I hope you allow yourself to feel the music. Enjoy its vibrancy, the exercise of dance, the hand-to-hand contact of a partner and the height of aliveness and survival. May you glide lightly over the dance floor, soak up the energetic vibration of the music while you feel the spiritual connection with your spouse, who has passed on, and recognize his blessing on you to get out there and *live*!

Dear Lord,
Thank you for listening to me; for showing me how to live; for placing special people in my life; for pointing out my blessings. But mostly, Lord, I thank you for not giving up on me. Thank you, for the joy of dancing through life. Amen.

My thoughts:

AMENDING DREAMS WORKBOOK

Dear Friend,

The purpose of this Workbook is to help you collect various aspects of your life that currently feel totally scattered, perhaps shattered, and out of control. By guiding you through some of the necessary aspects of getting these items organized, it is hoped that this Workbook will simplify your life. Feel free to take it to your appointments so you may jot down answers. In this way, most information you need is immediately accessible to you. However, should you carry it on your person, remember that it contains much of your personal confidential information, so safe precautions should be taken, such as:

a. Do not carry it everywhere, just when you know you will need it.

b. Keep it in a purse or briefcase so it is not obvious.

c. Store it in a safety deposit box in your home, or some hiding spot.

An additional benefit for completing this Workbook is that you will be providing your children, grandchildren, or whomever you name as beneficiaries in your Last Will and Testament, with a wealth of information to assist them when the time comes.

Remember that you are not alone. Unfortunately, there are many women in who find themselves sorting through the pieces of their lives to create their new life.

Please be good to yourself. Love yourself. Do one special thing for yourself every day. You deserve it. You have the right to it. You certainly are earning it. Maybe that something special is a chocolate raspberry latte, which you normally would not purchase. Perhaps you want to take an afternoon off from work or daily routines to simply sit in a park and read a book. Then you should do it.

Death reminds us that life is precious; that it does not go on forever in our present form. Very few things in life are extremely urgent, but many things are to be treasured.

PERSONAL INFORMATION

Name(s) I have been known by:

_____

_____

_____

Places I resided:

_____ From _____ to _____

_____ From _____ to _____

_____ From _____ to _____

_____ From _____ to _____

_____ From _____ to _____

My Social Security Number: _____-_____-_____

Listed under my name: _____.

My spouse's Social Security Number: _____-_____-_____

Location of my birth certificate: _____

Location of my marriage certificate: _____

Location of my spouse's birth certificate: _____

Location of your spouse's death certificate: _____

Additional Miscellaneous Notes:

_____

BURIAL LOCATIONS

Final burial/cremation plans for my death were made on _____,

_____ at _____

(Funeral Home)

Located at _____

(Street, City/Town, State, Zip Code)

Telephone No. (_____)_____-_____ or (_____)_____-_____

Refer to MEMORIAL/BURIAL REQUESTS for more details.

LOCATIONS OF REMAINS OF LOVED ONES:

Name:	Cemetery/Mausoleum	Site

BUDGET

Month: _____

Billed Items: *It is suggested that you complete 12 copies of this page—one for each month of the year. As some items (e.g., automobile license renewal, car inspection/registration) are only paid periodically, by planning for them in the month/year they become due, you will have the money set aside.)*

Keep a copy of paid bills with each monthly Budget sheet. In this way, should you need to locate the information, it will handy.

Rent/Mortgage Payment   Due Date: _____ $_____

Town/City & County Taxes   Due Date: _____ $_____

School Taxes   Due Date: _____ $_____

Automobile Payment   Due Date: _____ $_____

Auto Insurance   Due Date: _____ $_____

Inspection/Registration   Due Date: _____ $_____

License Renewal   Due Date: _____ $_____

Water   Due Date: _____ $_____

Gas & Electric   Due Date: _____ $_____

Oil   Due Date: _____ $_____

Propane   Due Date: _____ $_____

Trash Pickup   Due Date: _____ $_____

Newspaper   Due Date: _____ $_____

Newspaper   Due Date: _____ $_____

Magazine Subscription   Due Date: _____ $_____

Magazine Subscription   Due Date: _____ $_____

Charge Card _____   Due Date: _____ $_____

Charge Card _____   Due Date: _____ $_____

Charge Card _____   Due Date: _____ $_____

Charge Card _____   Due Date: _____ $_____

Bank Loan _____   Due Date: _____ $_____

Bank Loan _____   Due Date: _____ $_____

Cable: Due Date: _____ $_____

Internet: Due Date: _____ $_____

Telephone: Due Date: _____ $_____

Cellular Phone   Due Date: _____ $_____

Life Insurance   Due Date: _____ $_____

Life Insurance   Due Date: _____ $_____

Life Insurance   Due Date: _____ $_____

Medical Health Insurance   Due Date: _____ $_____

Dental Insurance   Due Date: _____ $_____

Misc.: _____   Due Date: _____ $_____

Misc.: _____   Due Date: _____ $_____

Misc.: _____   Due Date: _____ $_____

Misc.: _____   Due Date: _____ $_____

Misc.: _____   Due Date: _____ $_____

Misc.: _____   Due Date: _____ $_____

Misc.: _____   Due Date: _____ $_____

Misc.: _____   Due Date: _____ $_____
Misc.: _____   Due Date: _____ $_____
Misc.: _____   Due Date: _____ $_____
Misc.: _____   Due Date: _____ $_____
Misc.: _____   Due Date: _____ $_____
Misc.: _____   Due Date: _____ $_____
Misc.: _____   Due Date: _____ $_____
Misc.: _____   Due Date: _____ $_____
Misc.: _____   Due Date: _____ $_____
Misc.: _____   Due Date: _____ $_____

FINANCES

Perhaps you were not the spouse who wrote checks and, therefore, you have little knowledge of where the money went and what finances are available to you. The list below should help you begin to sort your finances. Should you not have some of these specifics, it would be good for you to search through a safety deposit box (at home or in a bank), desk drawer, or other storage areas where this information could be stored:

1. Income:

    a. Spouse's Employer—_____

       Human Resources Department Contact Person:

       _____

       Address: _____

       Telephone Number: _____

       E-Mail Address: _____

       Date of last check to be issued to you: _____

    b. My Employer—_____)_____

       Human Resources Department Contact Person:

       _____

       Address: _____

       Telephone Number: _____

       E-Mail Address: _____

2. Death Benefit: *Social Security Administration offers widows a one-time death benefit, if they are not of retirement age or already collecting Social Security. Your spouse's Human Resources Department should be able to provide*:

Social Security Administration nearest location: _____

_____

Contact Person: _____

Telephone Number: _____

3. Social Security Pension: (ask spouse's Human Resources Department)

    Location: _____

    Contact Person: _____

    Telephone Number: _____

    What is available to me?

_____

_____

_____

_____

_____

    When will it commence?

_____

_____

    What should I do in the meantime?

_____

_____

_____

_____

_____

4. Stocks: *Are you in possession of any Stock Certificates? If so, these are like having cash. In order to sell the stock, you will need to provide the original Stock Certificate.*

    Storage Location of Stock Certificates: _____

Name of Stock: _____

Number of Stock Shares: _____

Contact Person: _____

Contact Address: _____

Contact Phone: _____

Contact E-Mail: _____

Name of Stock: _____

Number of Stock Shares: _____

Contact Person: _____

Contact Address: _____

Contact Phone: _____

Contact E-Mail: _____

Name of Stock: _____

Number of Stock Shares: _____

Contact Person: _____

Contact Address: _____

Contact Phone: _____

Contact E-Mail: _____

Name of Stock: _____

Number of Stock Shares: _____

Contact Person: _____

Contact Address: _____

Contact Phone: _____

Contact E-Mail: _____

Name of Stock: _____

Number of Stock Shares: _____

Contact Person: _____

Contact Address: _____

Contact Phone: _____

Contact E-Mail: _____

Name of Stock: _____

Number of Stock Shares: _____

Contact Person: _____

Contact Address: _____

Contact Phone: _____

Contact E-Mail: _____

5. Bonds: Storage Location for bonds: _____

Bond denomination: _____   Maturity Date: _____

Bond denomination: _____   Maturity Date: _____

Bond denomination: _____   Maturity Date: _____

Bond denomination: _____   Maturity Date: _____

Bond denomination: _____   Maturity Date: _____

Bond denomination: _____   Maturity Date: _____

Bond denomination: _____   Maturity Date: _____

Bond denomination: _____   Maturity Date: _____

Bond denomination: _____   Maturity Date: _____

Bond denomination: _____   Maturity Date: _____

6. <u>Spouse's 401(k) or 403(b) **with current employer**</u>:

_____

Plan is handled by: _____

Address: _____

Telephone: _____

E-Mail: _____

Does it need to be rolled over? _____ If so, by what deadline? _____

Other important information: _____

_____

_____

_____

_____

_____

_____

<u>Spouse's **Former Employment** 401(k) or 403(b):</u>

Plan is handled by:_____

Address: _____

Telephone: _____

E-Mail: _____

Does it need to be rolled over? _____ If so, by what deadline? _____

Other important information: _____

_____

_____

_____

_____

_____

_____

My Former Employment 401(k) or 403(b):

Plan is handled by:: _____

Address: _____

Telephone: _____

E-Mail: _____

Does it need to be rolled over? _____ If so, by what deadline? _____

Other important information: _____

_____

_____

_____

_____

_____

_____

NOTE: You/your spouse's Banker _____ or Financial Advisor—_____ may have this information if you are unable to locate any paperwork at home or in your safety deposit box.

Safety Deposit Box(es):

Location: _____

Location: _____

Location: _____

Location: _____

Location: _____

There are more forms of investment, but these are the most common. If you have a financial advisor, that person should be contacted to explain what assets you possess and make suggestions as to how to make those assets work for you.

<u>*Other financial information*</u>:

Charge Account/Credit Cards:

Bill paid to: _____

Credit Card Number: _____

Payment Address: _____

Bill paid to: _____

Credit Card Number: _____

Payment Address: _____

Bill paid to: _____

Credit Card Number: _____

Payment Address: _____

Bill paid to: _____

Credit Card Number: _____

Payment Address: _____

Bill paid to: _____

Credit Card Number: _____

Payment Address: _____

Bill paid to: _____

Credit Card Number: _____

Payment Address: _____

<u>Current Real Estate</u>:

Property Address:

_____

Date of Purchase: _____

Mortgagee: _____

Location of Deed: _____

Location of Abstract of Title: _____

Title Insurance Company: _____

Attorney: _____

Property Address:

_____

Date of Purchase: _____

Mortgagee: _____

Location of Deed: _____

Location of Abstract of Title: _____

Title Insurance Company: _____

Attorney: _____

Property Address:

_____

Date of Purchase: _____

Mortgagee: _____

Location of Deed: _____

Location of Abstract of Title: _____

Title Insurance Company: _____

Attorney: _____

Property Address:

_____

Date of Purchase: _____

Mortgagee: _____

Location of Deed: _____

Location of Abstract of Title: _____

Title Insurance Company: _____

Attorney: _____

Property Address:

_____

Date of Purchase: _____

Mortgagee: _____

Location of Deed: _____

Location of Abstract of Title: _____

Title Insurance Company: _____

Attorney: _____

Property Address:

_____

Date of Purchase: _____

Mortgagee: _____

Location of Deed: _____

Location of Abstract of Title: _____

Title Insurance Company: _____

Attorney: _____

Property Address:

_____

Date of Purchase: _____

Mortgagee: _____

Location of Deed: _____

Location of Abstract of Title: _____

Title Insurance Company: _____

Attorney: _____

Property Address:

_____

Date of Purchase: _____

Mortgagee: _____

Location of Deed: _____

Location of Abstract of Title: _____

Title Insurance Company: _____

Attorney: _____

MEDICAL

Do you have a Health Care Proxy? *This document identifies the individual(s) whom you wish to make medical decisions for you should you be unable to do so for yourself. Either your medical doctor or attorney can provide you with the form, or you can search for one on the Internet. An attorney is not required for this document. If you have not signed one, please discuss it with your physician as soon as possible.*

Do you have a Living Will? *It makes know your wishes concerning your specific wishes concerning your medical treatment should you be unable to make decisions for yourself. A copy should be kept in your doctor's medical chart, in your safe deposit box, and with the named individual in your Health Care Proxy document.*

Primary Care Physician: _____

Address: _____

Telephone: _____

Emergency Number: _____

E-Mail: _____

Counselor/Psychiatrist: _____

Address: _____

Telephone: _____

Emergency Number: _____

E-Mail: _____

Dentist: _____

Address: _____

Emergency Number: _____

Telephone: _____

E-Mail: _____

Chiropractor: _____

Address: _____

Telephone: _____

E-Mail: _____

Specialist: _____

Address: _____

Telephone: _____

Emergency Number: _____

E-Mail: _____

Specialist: _____

Address: _____

Telephone: _____

Emergency Number: _____

E-Mail: _____

Specialist: _____

Address: _____

Telephone: _____

Emergency Number: _____

E-Mail: _____

Specialist: _____

Address: _____

Telephone: _____

Emergency Number: _____

E-Mail: _____

Your entire body is undergoing a tremendous amount of stress in dealing with the death of your spouse. It is most important that you take care of yourself, even if you do not feel like doing so. To assist you, here are some items to review:

1. Medical Health Insurance. If the HMO or other medical care insurance was a benefit of your spouse's employment, it is necessary to determine:

    a. Will my health coverage continue? _____

    b. How long will my health coverage be available to you? _____

    c. Will I have to pay part or the entire monthly premium? _____

    d. If I will have to pay a monthly premium, how much will it be? $_____

    e. If the health coverage will expire or has expired, ask spouse's employer what are my options, if any, through the company? _____

_____

_____

_____

_____

f. Am I eligible for Medicaid? _____

   If so, whom should I contact? _____

   Telephone Number: _____

g. Am I eligible for Medicare? _____

   If so, whom should I contact? _____

   Telephone Number: _____

h. Can I contact an organization offering medical health coverage to individuals—perhaps through the Chamber of Commerce, _____

i. What other organizations should I contact for health insurance program possibilities? _____

_____

_____

_____

_____

Current Medical Insurance Carrier_____

Address:_____

Telephone:_____

E-Mail: _____

_____

Policy Number: _____

2. Medical Conditions: Current medical conditions for which I am receiving doctor(s) care:

   a. _____

b. _____

c. _____

d. _____

e. _____

f. _____

g. _____

h. _____

i. _____

3. Medical Tests: List medical tests for which I have or need to make an appointment:

a. _____ date: _____ at_____

b. _____ date: _____ at_____

c. _____ date: _____ at_____

d. _____ date: _____ at_____

e. _____ date: _____ at_____

To refresh your memory, be sure to include:

☐ Sleep apnea follow-up

☐ Blood pressure check

☐ Appointment for medication adjustments or refills

☐ Counseling or psychiatric appointment

☐ Chemo or radiation treatments

☐ Levels to be checked for diabetes

☐ _____

☐ _____

☐ _____

☐ _____

☐ _____

☐ _____

☐ _____

☐ _____

☐ _____

☐ _____

4. Medical Appointments REMINDER for those I have scheduled:

√ With _____ on _____ at _____

√ With _____ on _____ at _____

√ With _____ on _____ at _____

√ With _____ on _____ at _____

√ With _____ on _____ at _____

5. Medicare: _____

6. Medicaid: _____

7. Extended Care Coverage:

Carrier: _____

Address: _____

Telephone: _____

E-Mail: _____

Notes concerning extended health care benefits:

_____

_____

_____

_____

_____

LEGAL DOCUMENTS

Assuming you have contacted your family attorney concerning what to do next, your attorney will review your spouse's Last Will and Testament, if one was executed. If you do not comprehend what the attorney is saying to you, ask that the question be worded differently until it is clear to you. Remember, you have just endured a traumatic experience, and your brain is not functioning at its normal capacity. The attorney should be receptive to your questions and be sensitive to your difficulty focusing on details at this time. You have the right to fully comprehend the legal details of your spouse's final wishes.

1. Last Will and Testament of Spouse/Estate:

If you have your spouse's original Last Will and Testament (or copy), bring it to your attorney. If there is no evidence of a Last Will and Testament, ask your spouse's attorney if one exists.

Some additional questions you may wish to ask include:

☐ Was there a trust fund? If so, what are the specifics?

☐ Is the house now entirely in my name now? If not, what needs to be done to put me in title?

☐ What assets owned solely by my spouse are now mine?

☐ What happens to any joint assets?

☐ Is there an Estate that needs to be probated? Please explain the process.

☐ How long does the Estate process take?

☐ What monies are tied up until the Estate is closed?

☐ What account(s) can I use until the Estate is closed?

☐ If I am the Executor of the Last Will and Testament, what are my obligations? Do I have to accept those obligations or can someone else undertake them, if I choose not to or do not feel qualified?

2. *Real Estate*: *Ask your attorney to explain the status of any real estate that is in the name of your spouse and/or your name real estate that is in the name of your spouse and/or your name. (Refer to page: _____—Real Estate)*

3. Trust: *Ask your attorney to explain any trust(s), which your spouse set up for you:*

In Name(s) of: _____

Handled by: _____

Address: _____

Telephone: _____

E-Mail: _____

INSURANCE

You should to notify your insurance agent of your spouse's passing. By removing your spouse from the policy(ies), you may be entitled to reimbursement of some paid premiums.

Car: Insurance agent: _____

       Address: _____

       Telephone: _____

       E-Mail: _____

       Contract Number: _____

Car Insurance Notes: _____

_____

_____

_____

_____

_____

Again, you will want to let the insurance agent know that the holder of the policy will be revised to your name.

Homeowners:

       Insurance agent: _____

       Address: _____

       Telephone: _____

       E-Mail: _____

       Contract Number: _____

Homeowners Insurance Notes: _____

_____

_____

_____

_____

_____

_____

If you have not already done so, contact your Life Insurance Agent to learn what your assets, rights and options are:

Life

Insurance agent: _____

Address: _____

Telephone: _____

E-Mail: _____

Contract Number: _____

Life Insurance Notes: _____

_____

_____

_____

_____

_____

MEMORIAL/BURIAL WISHES

Location of my Last Will and Testament: _____

Attorney: _____

Attorney's address: _____

Attorney's telephone: _____

Attorney's E-Mail: _____

Burial Arrangements Made in Advance at:

_____

Location: _____

I choose:

☐ Ground Burial   Location: _____

☐ Mausoleum   Location: _____

☐ Cremation

☐ Other: Describe: _____

I wish to have the following:

☐ Church Funeral: _____

☐ Funeral Chapel _____

☐ Gravesite Only _____

☐ Cemetery Chapel _____

☐ Other: _____

Additional wishes of mine include:

_____

_____

_____

_____

_____

_____

_____

Specifics for my funeral service, religious service, type of casket, headstone or inscription include:

_____

_____

_____

_____

_____

_____

_____

_____

_____

HOW CAN I SIMPLIFY MY LIFE?

As I mentioned, I was exhausted and it took several years to recognize that being responsible for housework, employment, shopping, cooking, laundry, errands, etc. was all on my shoulders.

Make a list of your weekly tasks:

1. _____

2. _____

3. _____

4. _____

5. _____

6. _____

7. _____

8. _____

9. _____

10. _____

11. _____

12. _____

13. _____

14. _____

15. _____

16. _____

17. _____

18. _____

19. _____

20. _____

Review your list. Which items could you do less frequently? (Highlight them in blue.) Which items could you pay someone to do? (Highlight them in green.) Which items absolutely must be accomplished weekly? (Highlight them in yellow.) If you have any items remaining, please determine which color-coding would best apply and highlight them accordingly.

Please use this list to organize your routines more efficiently.

May the Lord send his choicest blessings to you at this time. Amen.

978-0-595-36913-:
0-595-36913-8

Printed in the United States
40876LVS00007B/205-225

9 780595 369133